When the Lights Went Out

When the Lights Went Out

Three Studies on the Ancient Apostasy

Hugh W. Nibley

FOUNDATION FOR ANCIENT RESEARCH AND MORMON STUDIES (FARMS)
AT BRIGHAM YOUNG UNIVERSITY
PROVO, UTAH

Hugh W. Nibley (Ph.D., University of California, Berkeley) is Professor
Emeritus of History and Religion at Brigham Young University.

Cover design by Andrew Livingston

This collection was assembled and printed by Deseret Book Company, 1970.
These three articles also appear in *Mormonism and Early Christianity,* published
by the Foundation for Ancient Research and Mormon Studies and Deseret
Book Company, 1987.

Foundation for Ancient Research and Mormon Studies (FARMS)
Brigham Young University Institute for the Study and
Preservation of Ancient Religious Texts
P.O. Box 7113
University Station
Provo, Utah 84602

10 09 08 07 06 05 04 03 02 01   10 9 8 7 6 5 4 3 2 1

Library of Congress Cataloging-in-Publication Data

Nibley, Hugh, 1910–
     When the lights went out : three studies on the ancient Apostasy / Hugh W.
Nibley.
       p. cm.
     Includes bibliographical references and index.
     ISBN 0-934893-60-8
     1. Great Apostasy (Mormon doctrine) I. Title.
     BX8643.G74 N53 2001
     230'.9332—dc21

                                                         2001003393

Contents

Abbreviations

ANT   Montague R. James, *The Apocryphal New Testament* (Oxford: Clarendon, 1975)

NHL   James M. Robinson, ed., *The Nag Hammadi Library in English* (New York: Harper & Row, 1977)

OTP   James H. Charlesworth, ed., *The Old Testament Pseudepigrapha* (New York: Doubleday, 1983 and 1985)

PG   J.-P. Migne, ed., Patrologia graeca (Paris: Garnier, 1857–86)

PL   J.-P. Migne, ed., Patrologia latina (Paris: Garnier, 1844–64)

PO   François Nau and René Graffin, eds., Patrologia Orientalis (Paris: Librarie de Paris, firmin-Didot, 1903–)

1

The Passing of the Primitive Church: Forty Variations on an Unpopular Theme

A Somber Theme

Ever since Eusebius sought with dedicated zeal to prove the survival of the church by blazing a trail back to the apostles, the program of church history has been the same: "To give a clear and comprehensive, scientifically established view of the development of the visible institution of salvation founded by Christ."[1] To describe it—not to question it. By its very definition church history requires unquestioning acceptance of the basic proposition that the church did survive. One may write endlessly about the *Infant Church, l'Eglise naissante, die Pflanzung der Kirche,* etc., but one may not ask why the early Christians themselves described their church not as a lusty infant but as an old and failing woman; one may trace the triumphant spread of

"The Passing of the Church: Forty Variations on an Unpopular Theme" first appeared in *Church History* 20 (June 1961): 131–54. It was reprinted under the title "The Passing of the Primitive Church" in *When the Lights Went Out* (Salt Lake City: Deseret Book, 1970), 1–32. This article also appeared in *BYU Studies* 16 (1975): 139–64, and in *Mormonism and Early Christianity* (Salt Lake City: Deseret Book and FARMS, 1987), 168–208.

the *Unquenchable Light* through storm and shadow, but one
may not ask why Jesus himself insisted that the Light was to be
taken away.[2] Church history seems to be resolved never to raise
the fundamental question of survival as the only way of avoiding
a disastrous answer, and the normal reaction to the question—
did the church remain on earth?—has not been serious inquiry
in a richly documented field but shocked recoil from the edge
of an abyss into which few can look without a shudder.[3]

Yet today that question is being asked again, as it has been
in other times of stress and crisis, not with the journalistic
flourish of Soltau's *Sind wir noch Christen?* but with the cautious historical appraisal of a Hans J. Schoeps, contemplating
the age-old tension between eschatology and church with their
conflicting ideas about the church's future. Can it be that the
repugnance of churchmen to eschatology and their coolness
toward the authentic writings of the early fathers are due in no
small part to the dim view which the primitive Christians took
of the prospects of the church?[4] The purpose of this paper is to
list briefly the principal arguments supporting the thesis that
the church founded by Jesus and the apostles did not survive
and was not expected to. We shall consider the fate of the
church under three heads: (a) the declarations of the early
Christians concerning what was to befall it; (b) their strange
behavior in the light of those declarations; (c) the affirmations
and denials, doubts and misgivings of the church leaders of a
later day. Our *theme* is the passing of the church; our *variations,* designated below by parenthetical numbers, are an abun-
dance of striking and often neglected facets of church history.

The Early Christian View

Christian apologists had a ready answer to those shallow-
minded critics who made merry over Christ's failure to convert
the world and God's failure to protect his saints from persecution

and death: God does not work that way, it was explained; his rewards are on the other side, and his overwhelming intervention is reserved for the *eschaton,* until which all sorts of reverses can be expected—*nihil enim est nobis promissum ad hanc vitam;* the prospect of failure and defeat in the world, far from being incompatible with the gospel message, is an integral part of it.[5]

(1) Jesus announced in no uncertain terms that his message would be rejected by all men, as the message of the prophets had been before,[6] and that he would soon leave the world to die in its sins and seek after him in vain.[7] The light was soon to depart, leaving a great darkness "in which no man can work," while "the prince of this world" would remain, as usual, in possession of the field.[8] (2) In their turn the disciples were to succeed no better than their Lord: "If they have called the master of the house Beelzebub, how much more shall they call them of his household?"[9] Like him they were to be "hated of all men," going forth as sheep among wolves, "sent last as it were appointed unto death,"[10] with the promise that as soon as they completed their mission the end would come.[11]

(3) But what of the church? Those who accepted the teaching were to suffer exactly the same fate as the Lord and the apostles; they were advised to "take . . . the prophets . . . for an example of suffering affliction and of patience," and to "think it not strange concerning the fiery trial which is to try" them, but rejoice rather to suffer as Christ did "in the flesh . . . that we may be also glorified together."[12] After them too the prince of this world was waiting to take over; they too were to be lambs among wolves, rejected as were the Master and the disciples: "The world knoweth us not because it knew him not."[13] Knowing that "whosoever will save his life must lose it," they openly disavowed any expectation of success, individual or collective, in this world.[14] (4) As for the doctrine, it was to receive the same

rough treatment, soon falling into the hands of worldly men who would pervert the gospel of Christ from a thing the world found highly obnoxious to something it was willing to embrace, for such has always been the fate of God's revelations to men.[15]

(5) All this bodes ill for the interval between the ascension and the parousia, or second coming; the *Zwischenzeit* was to be a bad time and a long one.[16] What is more, it begins almost immediately, the apostles themselves calling attention to all the fatal signs, and marveling only that it has come so soon.[17] As soon as the Lord departs there comes "the lord of this world, and hath nothing in me"; in the very act of casting out the Lord of the vineyard the usurpers seize it for themselves, to remain in possession until his return;[18] no sooner does he sow his wheat than the adversary sows tares, and only when the Lord returns again can the grain be "gathered together," that is, into a church, the ruined field itself being not the church but specifically "the world."[19] After the sheep come the wolves, "not sparing the flock," which enjoys no immunity (Acts 20:29); after sound doctrine come fables;[20] after the charismatic gifts only human virtues (1 Corinthians 13:8, 13). The list is a grim one, but it is no more impressive than (6) the repeated insistence that *there is to be an end,* not the end of the world, but "the consummation of the age."[21] It is to come with the completion of the missionary activities of the apostles, and there is no more firmly rooted tradition in Christendom than the teaching that the apostles completed the assigned preaching to the nations in their own persons and in their own time, so that the end could come in their generation.[22]

(7) It was no imaginary end. When the saints were asked to "endure to the end," that meant just one thing, as Tertullian observes—to suffer death.[23] When the sorely pressed Christians need "a strong comfort," the only comfort forthcoming is the

promise of the resurrection and the assurance of salvation
"whether we live or die."[24] Never is there any mention of relief
on the way, of happy times ahead, of final victory for the cause,
or of the consoling thought that generations yet unborn will
call one blessed. Such assurances belong to a later age; the only
encouragement the first Christians ever got is that given to soldiers making a last-ditch stand: they are ordered not to attack
but "to have long patience," grimly hanging on "to the end,"
because only by so doing can they show their worthiness to
inherit eternal life.[25]

But we are told not only of one but explicitly of *two* ways
in which the ancient church was to make its exit. (8) For far
more numerous than those true saints who were to give their
lives as witnesses were those who were to succumb to the blandishments of false teachers. The fate of the vast majority of
Christians was not to be overcome by a frontal attack—true
martyrs were relatively few—but to be led astray by perverters.[26] The spoilers do not destroy the vineyard but "seize the
inheritance" for themselves; we read of betrayal, disobedience,
corruptions; of deceivers, perverters, traitors; of wresting the
scriptures, denying the gifts, quenching the Spirit, turning love
into hate, truth to fables, sheep to wolves; of embracing "another gospel," and so forth. The offenders are not pagans but
loudly professing Christians.[27] As, once the prophets are dead,
everyone paints their tombs with protestations of devotion, so
"when the master of the house has risen up and shut the door,"
shall the eager host apply for admission to his company—too
late.[28] The apostasy described in the New Testament is not *de-
sertion* of the cause, but *perversion* of it, a process by which "the
righteous are removed, and none perceives it."[29] The Christian
masses do not realize what is happening to them; they are
"bewitched" by a thing that comes as softly and insidiously as

the slinging of a noose.[30] It is an old familiar story, as Rudolf Bultmann notes: "The preaching of Jesus does not hold out any prospect for the future of the people. . . . The present people does not behave otherwise than its predecessors who had persecuted and killed the prophets. . . . The message of Jesus does not contain any promise of the splendid future of Israel."[31] (9) As is well known, the early Christians viewed the future with a mixture of fear and longing, of longing for the triumphant return of the Lord but of deadly fear of the long and terrible rule of the *cosmoplanēs* that had to come first. So great is the dread of what they know lies ahead, that devout fathers of the church pray for the indefinite postponement of the Day of the Lord itself as the price of delaying the rule of darkness.[32]

(10) The apostolic fathers denounce with feeling the all too popular doctrine that God's church simply cannot fail. All past triumphs, tribulations, and promises, they insist, will count for nothing unless the people now repent and stand firm in a final test that lies just ahead; God's past blessings and covenants, far from being a guarantee of immunity (as many fondly believe) are the very opposite, for "the greater the knowledge we have received, the greater rather is the danger in which we lie."[33] The case of the Jews, to say nothing of the fallen angels, should prove that we are never safe.[34] God will surely allow his people to perish if they continue in the way they are going—he will hasten their dissolution: "Since I called and ye hearkened not . . . therefore I in my turn will laugh at your destruction. . . . For there will come a time when you will call upon me and I shall not hear you."[35] The apostolic fathers compare the church to fallen Israel and confirm their solemn warnings by citing the most lurid and uncompromising passages of scripture.[36] (11) They see the church running full speed in the wrong direction and in great distress of mind plead with it to do an about-face

"before it is too late," as it soon will be.[37] For their whole concern is not to make new converts but rather "to save from perishing a soul that has already known Christ," seeing to it that as many as possible pass "the fiery test ahead," keep the faith that most are losing, and so reach the goal of glory beyond.[38] They know that the names of Christ and Christian carry on but find no comfort in that since those names are being freely used by impostors and corrupters,[39] whom "the many" are gladly following.[40]

(12) The call to repentance of the apostolic fathers is a last call; they labor the doctrine of the Two Ways as offering to Christian society a last chance to choose between saving its soul by dying in the faith or saving its skin by coming to terms with the world.[41] They have no illusions as to the way things are going: the church has lost the gains it once made, the people are being led by false teachers,[42] there is little to hinder the fulfillment of the dread (and oft-quoted) prophecy, "the Lord shall deliver the sheep of his pasture and their fold and their tower to destructions."[43] The original tower with its perfectly cut and well-fitted stones is soon to be taken from the earth, and in its place will remain only a second-class tower of defective stones which could not pass the test.[44] In the *Visions* of the Shepherd of Hermas, the church is represented as an old and failing lady—"because your spirit is old and already fading away"—who is carried out of the world; only in the world beyond does she appear as a blooming and ageless maiden.[45] The apostolic fathers take their leave of a church not busily engaged in realizing the kingdom but fast falling asleep; the lights are going out, the Master has departed on his long journey, and until he returns all shall sleep. What lies ahead is the Wintertime of the Just, the time of mourning for the Bridegroom, when men shall seek the Lord and not find him, and "seek to do good, but no longer be able to."[46]

Strange Behavior

What the strangely negative behavior of the first Christians suggests is less the expectation of an immediate parousia than the shutting up of the shop until a distant reopening. (13) It has often been noted that their public relations were the world's worst, that they "could not and did not court publicity outside the movement."[47] In sharp contrast to the later church, they were convinced, as Hilary observes, that the church "could not be Christ's unless the world hated it."[48] The disciples, following the example and precept of their Master, made no effort to win public sympathy and support.[49] This hard and uncompromising attitude has puzzled observers in every age, and indeed it makes little sense in an institution seeking either to convert the world or to survive in it.[50] None knew better than the Christians themselves that their intransigence had no survival value, and yet they went right on "turning the world upside down" and mortally offending respectable people.

(14) The first Christians maintained a strange and stubborn reticence on certain matters (including their beliefs about the second coming), even when their silence led to serious misunderstanding and persecution.[51] Even among the members the teaching was carefully rationed, for it was not the trivia but the high and holy mysteries, the most prized things of the kingdom, that were carefully kept out of circulation,[52] so that Origen can report no clear official teaching in his day "not only regarding minor matters, but on the very first principles of the gospel."[53] Critics and scholars since Celsus have been puzzled by this early Christian reticence on matters which, if the church was to carry on, should have been highly publicized.[54] And while Christians since Irenaeus have categorically denied that any teachings of the apostolic church were withheld, they

have done so only to avoid the alarming implications of the primitive Christian reticence.[55]

(15) Consistent with the policy of reticence is the strict limitation placed on the missionary activities of Jesus and his disciples, both in time and place, and their firm rejection of the highly successful proselytizing methods of the Jews. In his recent study of this anomaly, Joachim Jeremias has concluded that while Jesus did indeed envisage a universal call to the nations, he thought of it as coming only at the *eschaton* and not at the time of his mortal mission, which clearly did not have world conversion as its objective.[56]

(16) No less striking is the conspicuous absence of any missionary organization in the apostolic church and the complete indifference of the apostolic fathers to the great business of converting the world.[57] Their prayer for the church is to be gathered *out* of the world, not spread abroad in it, and to be caught up into the kingdom, not to build it here.[58]

(17) Instead of settling down as the later Christians sensibly did to long-term projects of conversion, the early Christians were driven by the "keen sense of urgency and stress" that fills their writings. "The time is short" was the refrain, and the missionaries had only time to give a hasty warning message and be on their way. It seems, according to K. Holl, that the apostles went about their business *ohne für die Zukunft zu sorgen*—without a thought for the future.[59] What strange missionaries! They never speak of the bright future ahead nor glory in its prospects but seem quite prepared to accept the assurance that they would preach to a generation that would not hear them and that, as in the days of Noah, the end would follow hard upon their preaching.[60]

(18) But if the early saints mention no glorious future for the church, when that should be their strongest comfort, they

do shed abundant tears when they look ahead. If the fall of Jerusalem and the temple was to be the great opportunity for the church that later theologians insist it was, Christ and the early saints were not aware of it, for they give no indication of regarding the event as anything but tragic.[61] Paul viewed the future of the church "with tears" as, according to early accounts, did other leaders.[62] Apocryphal writings describe the apostles as weeping inconsolably when Jesus leaves them to their fates, and in turn the church shedding bitter tears for the loss of the apostles, leaving it without guidance and counsel.[63] Whatever their historical value, such accounts convincingly convey a mood, and Kirsopp Lake recommended Browning's terrible *Death in the Desert* as the best background reading for understanding the state of mind of the church at the passing of the apostles—all is lost.[64]

(19) The failure of the apostles to leave behind them written instructions for the future guidance of the church has often been noted and sadly regretted. It is hard to conceive of such a colossal oversight if the founders had actually envisaged a long future for the church. The awkwardness of the situation is apparent from Robert M. Grant's explanation of it, namely, that the apostles "did not live to see the Church fully organized and at work."[65] As if they should wait until the work was completed before giving instructions for completing it![66] Actually the most tragic disorganization and confusion followed hard upon the passing of the apostles, according to Hegesippus, and as a direct result of it. Plainly the early leaders made no careful provision for the future, even as they "failed to compose anything that could properly be described as 'church-history'" in spite of their great interest in times, seasons, and dispensations and the imperative need and accepted use of sacred history in the economy of religious organizations.[67]

(20) Then there is the total neglect of education in the early church, which Gustave Bardy would justify with desperate logic, arguing that education for the young was neglected because the church got its membership from converts among the adult population—*fiunt, non nascuntur Christiani.*[68] And were all those converts childless, and were there no children in the church for those three long centuries during which it was without schools? In view of the great emphasis placed on education by the church in the fourth century, its total neglect in the preceding centuries can only have been deliberate. Well might Eugéne de Faye find it strange that Jesus "ne songe nullement à former une école de jeunes hommes qui . . . seraient les hérétiers de sa doctrine" (does not think to form a school of young men who would be the heirs of his teaching), for if there were to be heirs of the teaching such a provision was indispensable.[69] Why no education, then? Actually the apostolic fathers were greatly concerned about education, warning their people against the bad education of the world and chiding them for their neglect of the only education that counted—that which prepared the young for the next life.[70]

(21) Neglect of standard education was matched by an equally disturbing indifference to the social and political problems which would necessarily be of vital concern to any enduring social institution. For years liberal scholars sought to discover a social gospel where none was to be found, and it is indeed hard to believe that a religion of brotherly love could so persistently ignore the crying social ills of the day.[71] But the Christians excused themselves with the explanation that more urgent business had priority—they had no *time* for such things.[72] Why not, if the church was to continue? (22) And why should a permanent and growing church refuse to invest in lands and buildings? For a long time eminent churchmen endorsed

the old Christian prejudice against the construction of sorely needed church buildings.[73] But what could have been the original objection to anything as innocent and salutary as the building of a church? The early Christians tell us: the church cannot own real estate (they explain) because it is only here temporarily, and it must never be allowed to forget that fact.[74] (23) Hans Lietzmann has shown that when "the Church sojourning at Rome" or elsewhere writes to "the Church sojourning at Corinth" or elsewhere it means that both churches are thought of only as temporary visitors in their cities; collectively and individually the church was here only on a brief pilgrimage. They were *das wandernde Gottesvolk,* strangers and pilgrims all, destined for but a short time upon the earth.[75]

Planned Martyrdom

The strongest argument for the survival of the church is the natural reluctance of men to accept defeat—even temporary defeat—for the work of God: "Tot denique martyria in vacuum coronata?" cries Tertullian, ignoring Polycarp's assurance that "all of these ran not in vain, because they are with the Lord in the place which is their due, with whom they also suffered. For they did not love this present world."[76] (24) The loudly proclaimed objectives of the first martyrs do not include the future prosperity of the church. In bidding farewell to Jews and Gentiles, Paul announces that his missions to them have been successful, not in terms of converts, but of clearing himself of a terrible responsibility: henceforth their blood is on their own heads; he has fulfilled his assignment successfully, for a crown awaits him—on the other side.[77] "Thus it appears," writes Oscar Cullmann, "that the coming of the Kingdom does not depend upon the success of this 'preaching' but only on the fact of the proclamation itself."[78] What does depend on the preaching is (a) the salvation of the preacher, who is under condemnation unless he bears witness and frees himself of "the blood of this generation," and (b) the convicting of a wicked world which must be "without excuse" in the day of judgment.[79] The preaching is not to convert the world but "for a witness"—*martyria* occurs more than six times as frequently as *kerygma* in the New Testament—and it has long been recognized that the primary qualification and calling of an apostle was to be an eyewitness.[80] The calling of a witness is to preach to an unbelieving generation ripe for destruction, with the usual expectation (as the name "martyr" indicates) of being rejected and put to death.

(25) The strange indifference of the early martyrs to the future of a church for which later ages fondly believed they gave their lives has not received the comment it deserves. In a world in which a noble altruism was constantly on the lips of orators, in a society whose model citizen was that Pius Aeneas who promised his afflicted followers that grateful generations to come would call them blessed, and in a sect which placed brotherly love before all else, the Christian martyrs, unlike the pagan martyrs or Christian heroes of later times, never take comfort in the thought that others will profit by their sufferings, or that their deeds will be remembered and their names revered in ages to come. Ignatius, Andrew, and Perpetua will neither live nor die for the church but talk of nothing but their personal glory with Christ hereafter, "for while he suffered for us, we suffer for ourselves."[81] This concept of martyrdom is the opposite of that which later prevailed, as Dionysius of Alexandria points out in a letter to Novatus, noting that whereas the early martyr was concerned "for his own soul alone . . . today the martyr thinks in terms of the whole Church."[82] Since the latter is the more humane and natural view, there must have been a very good reason for ignoring it. It could not have

been that primitive Christians enjoyed suffering, for they did not;[83] nor were they as self-centered even as the later Christians, who found in martyrdom the solace of matchless public acclaim and undying earthly renown.[84] The very tears of the early leaders show plainly enough (as Chrysostom often observes) that they were genuinely concerned about the future. If, then, the martyrs refuse to think and speak in terms of a continuing church, it is not because they are peculiarly self-centered people, but simply because they see no future for the church.

(26) So firmly fixed in the Christian mind is the conviction that every true Christian, every saint, is by very definition a martyr, that when persecutions ceased devout souls felt themselves cheated, and new ways and means of achieving martyrdom had to be devised, though they were never more than substitutes for the real thing.[85] A telling argument for any sect seeking to prove its authenticity has ever been the claim to have more martyrs than the others,[86] while the largest church of all at the peak of its power must needs describe itself in pathetic terms as a persecuted little band of saints—for tradition will not allow any other kind of church to be the true one.[87] From the beginning the church is a community of martyrs, whose proper business is "nothing else than to study how to die";[88] and though "the final note is of the victory of God," as Clarence T. Craig observes, before that happy culmination John "seems to have anticipated a universal martyrdom for the Church."[89]

The Great Gap

That ominous gap in the records which comes just at the moment of transition from a world-hostile to a world-conditioned Christianity has recently received growing attention and a number of interesting labels, such as the lacuna, the eclipse, the void, the great vacuum, the narrows, the period of oblivion, etc.[90] S. G. F. Brandon compares it to a tunnel "from which we emerge to find a situation which is unexpected in terms of the situation which went before."[91] (27) The church, that is, which comes out of the tunnel is *not* the church that went into it. The great gap is more than a mere absence of documents; it is an abrupt break in the continuity of the church, so complete as to prove to Theodore Brandt that "the living faith cannot be transmitted from past ages," which is at least an admission that it has not been.[92] The early Christians knew they were approaching a tunnel; they were acutely aware of "the terrible possibility of apostasy for the church"—not merely of apostasy *from* it[93]— and never doubted "the general apostasy which would precede the coming of the Messiah."[94] And the church of the next age is just as aware of having passed through the tunnel and losing its more precious possessions in the process. (28) For after the passing of the apostles "le vide est immense" (the void is immense), since it was the presence of living witnesses that had made the original church what it was.[95] Henceforth the "elders" of old are referred to as a fabulous race of beings endowed with gifts, powers, and knowledge far exceeding anything found on earth any more, and mere proximity to the apostles and the elders becomes a special mark of sanctity and authority.[96] As "the great lights went out" the most devoted Christians engaged in a wistful "Operation Salvage" to rescue what might still be saved of "those things which came by the living voices that yet remained."[97] What more eloquent commentary on the passing of the church?

(29) At the same time a horde of deceivers, "who up until then had been lurking in dark corners," as soon as they saw that there were no more apostles left to call them to account, came boldly forth, each claiming that he alone had the gnosis which the Lord had secretly imparted to the apostles after the resurrection.[98] Strangely, they met with no official opposition: the

fathers who oppose them emphatically disclaim any apostolic authority and, what is more, know of no one else who might have it.[99] "Nous sommes incapable," writes D. Busy, "d'expliquer comment, la terre entière se trouvant évangélisée, les prédicateurs de l'évangile ont l'air de disparaître et laissent le champ libre aux faux méssies et aux faux prophètes; comme . . . la bête de la mer ne rencontre plus la moindre résistance" (We are unable to explain how, while the whole was being evangelized, the preachers of the gospel seem to disappear and leave the field free for false messiahs and false prophets; how . . . the beast of the sea does not meet the least resistance).[100] The prophecy (2 Thessalonians 2:2–3) is no more puzzling than the event; for the second century, the great moment of transition, is no age of faith but "par excellence the age of Heresy."[101]

It was not a case of reformers or schismatics attacking the main church—the problem was, since the Christians had always rejected with contempt the argument of mere numbers, to find the true church among a great number of sects, each claiming to be the one true original article and displaying facsimiles of ancient spiritual gifts, rites, and officers to prove it.[102] Justin knows of no certain norm for distinguishing true Christians from false, and Irenaeus struggles manfully but vainly to discover one.[103] While the perplexed masses asked embarrassing questions and flocked to the banner of any quack who gave promise of possessing the gifts and powers, especially prophecy, which it was commonly felt the church should have inherited,[104] even the greatest churchmen hesitated and wavered, unable to resist the appeal of the old charismatic Christianity or to decide just where it was to be found.[105] In the end, in Adolf von Harnack's words, "Gnosticism won half a victory," for if the "Gnostics-so-called" had to default on electrifying promises which they could not fulfill, neither was any found to match their false claims with the genuine article, and the great surge of hope and enthusiasm that had carried the gnostics on its crest subsided in disillusionment and compromise.[106]

(30) Still, the constant revival through the centuries of the old stock gnostic claim that the one true apostolic church has by some miracle of survival come down to the possession of this or that group, is a perpetual reminder of the failure of subsequent Christianity to come up to the expectations of the first church.[107] (31) For the chronic discontent which haunts the Christian churches is by no means limited to the lunatic fringe. The vigorous beginnings of monasticism and pilgrimage were frankly attempts to return to the first order of the church, with its unworldly austerities and its spiritual manifestations, and as such were viewed by official Christianity as a clear vote of no-confidence—a rebuke and repudiation of the system.[108]

(32) Modern students have agreed in describing the second generation of the church as a time of spiritual decline and low vitality, of torpor and exhaustion, "a dull period of feeble originality and a dearth of great personalities."[109] "Enfin," writes Bardy, "c'est le tiedeur que domine."[110] Doctrinally it was a definite "Abfall vom Evangelium," with the basic teachings altered and denatured beyond recognition.[111] As "the understanding of the Spirit . . . became lost . . . and the Christian had to rely on his own powers," that Christian became calculating, complacent, and respectable, in a word, all that the first Christian was not.[112] The overall impression, Maurice Goguel reports, is "definitely one of decadence."[113]

Yet the same voices that bring these charges against the second generation unanimously approve the new mentality as a necessary coming down out of the clouds, a new-found sobriety and maturity, a sensible acceptance of the facts of life, as "uplifted eyes . . . [turned back] to earth . . . to find their assurance in hard facts."[114] At last, we are told, the Christian could enjoy "what he had been missing so long, the consideration and respect of the outside world."[115] Only by scrapping the old "evangelical eschatology," according to one Catholic authority, could "Christian morality and the Church itself ... take on larger dimensions," this being (according to another) a necessary step "towards wider horizons than those to which the Galilean nucleus had chosen to confine itself."[116] One may well ask how wider horizons and larger dimensions could be achieved by a Christianity admittedly "more hard and fast, less spontaneous, and in a sense, more cramped" than what had gone before; Johannes de Zwaan, who describes it thus, marvels "that the main stream of Gospel-tradition could pass through these narrows."[117] But the larger dimensions were the intellectual splendors of Hellenism, toward which the gnostic agitation had hurried the feet of the church, the new Christian culture substituting erudition for inspiration, the rhetoric of the schools for the gift of tongues, a *numerus episcoporum* for the *Spiritus per spiritalem hominem*,[118] and the orderly mechanics of ritual for the unpredictable operation of the spiritual gifts as "eschatological consciousness changed into sacramental piety."[119] "Christianity," wrote Wilhelm Christ, "was squeezed into a system congenial to pagan-Greek-rationalist thought, and in that safe protective suit of armor was able to face up to the world; but in the process it had to sacrifice its noblest moral and spiritual forces."[120] In paying the stipulated price for survival, the church of the second century proved what the early church knew so well, that whosoever would save his life must lose it.[121]

(33) The sensational change from the first to the second generation of the church was not, as it is usually depicted, a normal and necessary step in a long steady process of evolution. It was radical and abrupt, giving the old Christianity

when set beside the new "tout l'aspect d'une anomalie," as Louis Duchesne puts it—an anomaly so extreme that many scholars have doubted that the primitive church ever existed.[122] "Rapidity of evolution explains the difference between the gospels and the second century," we are assured.[123] But rapidity is the sign not of evolution but of revolution, and the second-century upheaval was no part of a continuing trend at all, for after that one tremendous shift there are no more such changes of course in the way of the church: henceforward fundamental attitudes and concepts remain substantially unchanged.[124] Eduard Norden has noted that early Christian literature had no literary predecessors and no successors but appears as a completely alien intrusion into the classical tradition, an incongruous and unwelcome interruption, an indigestible lump which, however, disappears as suddenly as it came, leaving the schoolmen to resume operations as if nothing had happened.[125] The march of civilization continued, but it was not the march of the church.

Arguments for Survival

The arguments put forth by those who would prove the survival of the church are enough in themselves to cast serious doubts upon it. (34) The first thing that strikes one is the failure of the ingenuity of scholarship to discover any serious scriptural support for the thesis. There are remarkably few passages in the Bible that yield encouragement even to the most determined exegesis, and it is not until centuries of discussion have passed that we meet with the now familiar interpretations of the "mustard seed" and "gates-of-hell" imagery, which some now hold to be eschatological teachings having no reference whatever to the success of the church on earth.[126]

The most effective assertions of survival are the rhetorical ones. We have already referred to the subtle use of such loaded terms as the *Infant Church,* the *Unquenchable Light,* etc., which merely beg the question. Equally effective is the "quand même" (even though) argument, which frankly admits the exceedingly dim prospects of the early church and the scant possibility of survival and then, without further explanation, announces in awed and triumphant tones: "But in spite of everything it *did* survive!" (35) Survival is admittedly a miracle and a paradox; its very incredibility is what makes it so wonderful.[127] Ecstatic assertion alone carries the day where any serious discussion of evidence would mark one a cavilling cynic, for this argument comes right out of the schools of rhetoric; its favorite image, that of the storm-tossed ship which somehow never sinks because it bears virtuous souls, is already a commonplace in the Roman schools of declamation.[128] The thrilling voices that assure us that all the powers of evil rage in vain are not those of the early fathers, but of imperial panegyrists and spell-binding bishops of another day, with their comforting pronouncements that God has, as it were, invested so heavily in his church that he simply would not think of letting it fail at this late date.[129]

The strongest support of this "facile and dangerous optimism" has always been the decisive fact of survival itself, as proven by the undiminished eminence of the Christian name; only, in fact, if one defines apostasy as "a more or less express renunciation" of that name can the survival of the church be taken for granted, as it generally is.[130] But what is the authority of the Christian label when early apologists can declare that it has become meaningless in their time, being as freely employed by false as by true Christians?[131] Or when the apostolic fathers protest that vast numbers "bear the name deceitfully"? Or when Jesus himself warns that "many shall come in *my* name," and all of them falsely: "Believe none of them!"[132]

A favorite theme of fiction and drama has ever been the stirring victory of Christianity over all the powers and blandishments of paganism. But this was victory over a straw man, a papier-mâché dragon brought onto the stage to prove to a confused and doubting world that the right had been victorious after all.[133] The early leaders worried constantly, and only, about the enemy within; paganism, long dead on its feet, the butt of the schoolmen for centuries, was not the real enemy at all. (36) There were, to be sure, areas of doctrine and ritual in which paganism did present a real threat, but precisely there the church chose to surrender to the heathen, the pious economy of whose splendid festivals and the proud preeminence of whose venerated schools became an integral part of the Christian heritage.[134]

Christians have often taken comfort in the axiom that it is perfectly unthinkable that God should allow his church to suffer annihilation, that he would certainly draw the line somewhere. This is the very doctrine of ultimate immunity against which the apostolic fathers thunder, and later fathers remind us that we may not reject the appalling possibility simply because it is appalling.[135] (37) If wicked men can "kill the Prince of Peace" and Belial enjoy free reign as "the prince of this world," where is one to draw the line at what is unthinkable? For Hilary the suggestion that Jesus actually wept is baffling, paradoxical, and unthinkable—"yet he wept!"[136] If "after the prophets came the false prophets, and after the Apostles the false apostles, and after the Christ the Antichrist," is it unthinkable that the church should likewise have a dubious successor?[137] After all, Christians like Jerome found it quite unthinkable that Rome could ever fall and used identical arguments to affirm the ultimate impregnability of the church and the empire.[138] The hollowness of the rhetorical arguments for sure survival has become apparent in times of world calamity, when the orators themselves have, like Basil and Chrysostom, suddenly reverted to the all-but-forgotten idiom of apocalyptic and eschatology and asked, "Is it not possible that the Lord has already deserted us entirely?"[139] The question is the more revealing for being uttered with heavy reluctance and in times of deepest soul-searching.

(38) How deeply rooted in Christian thinking was the belief that the church would pass away is seen in the remarkable insistence of the orators of the fourth century that the great victory of the church, which at that time took everyone by surprise, was actually a *restoration* of the church, which had passed away entirely: "We of the church were not half-dead but wholly dead and buried in our graves," the apostasy and the age of darkness had actually come as predicted, and were now being followed, as prophesied, by a new day of restoration.[140] Here was an explanation that fitted the traditional view of the future: the church, it was explained, is like the moon, a thing that disappears and reappears from time to time.[141] But if the fourth-century triumph was really that "restitution of all things" foretold by the apostle (Acts 3:21), it could only betoken the arrival of the *eschaton,* and so the orators duly proclaimed the dawn of the millennial day and the coming of the New Jerusalem.[142]

(39) One of the most significant things about "the glorious and unexpected triumph of the Church" was precisely that it *was* unexpected; everybody was surprised and puzzled by it.[143] It was not what people had been taught to expect, and the remedy for their perplexity was a bold revamping of the story: "The facts speak for themselves," is Chrysostom's appeal,[144] and Eusebius sets his hand to a new kind of church history, with success—easy, inevitable success—as his theme.[145] Traditional

concepts were quickly and radically overhauled. The familiar Two Ways were no longer the ways of light and darkness lying before Israel or the church, but the way of the church itself: Our church, versus the way of the opposition, whoever they might be.[146] "To endure to the end" no longer meant to suffer death but the opposite—to outlive one's persecutors and enjoy one's revenge.[147] The old warnings and admonitions were given a new and optimistic twist: "As it was in the days of Noah" now meant that all was well, since "the rains did not come until Noah was safely in the Ark";[148] "No man knows the hour" becomes a *cura solicitudinis,* a comforting assurance that there was plenty of time and no need to worry;[149] "this generation shall not pass away" really meant that the generations of the church would *never* pass away.[150] It did not disturb a generation bred on rhetoric to be told that Peter heard with amazement that one should forgive seventy times seven, that being an announcement of the future generations that should believe.[151] Nor did it seem overbold to explain the prediction that the apostles should be hated of all men as a rhetorical exaggeration;[152] or to interpret the Lord's prediction that men would seek him in vain as proof of his presence in the church, which would render any searching a waste of time, that is, vain;[153] for it is *not* the Lord but the devil who comes "as a thief in the night."[154]

One might fill a book with examples of such bold and clever rhetoric: the presence of wolves in the church simply fulfills the millennial promise that the wolf and the lamb shall graze together;[155] tares in the church are a sign of its divinity, since it must embrace all men, good and bad, to be God's church.[156] What really happened was that the sheep promptly routed the wolves and the wheat overcame the tares—not the other way around![157] It was easy to show that all the bad predictions were duly fulfilled—on the heads of the Jews—while all the good promises made to *them* were properly meant for the Christians. The tears of the apostles were actually the happiest of omens for the church, exciting in all beholders, by a familiar rhetorical trick, those feelings of pity and devotion which would guarantee unflinching loyalty to the cause forever.[158] It is fascinating to see how Chrysostom can turn even the most gloomy and depressing reference to the future of the church into a welcome promise of survival: the very fact that the ancient saints *worried* about things to come proves that there was to be a future, and so—delightful paradox!—they had nothing to worry about![159] If it can be said of the orating bishops that "the true size and color of every object is falsified by the exaggerations of their corrupt eloquence,"[160] it must also be noted that these were not wanton or irresponsible men but devoted leaders desperately desirous of assuring themselves and their people of the unassailable integrity of the church: Chrysostom repeatedly declares that the church is higher, holier, and (above all) more enduring than heaven itself.[161] He could do that (on the authority of Luke 21:33) without a blush because rhetoric had transferred the church into a glorious abstraction, a noble allegory, and as such an eternal, spiritual, indestructible entity.[162] On the other hand he *had* to do it to meet the importunities of those who beset him night and day "unceasingly and everlastingly" with searching and embarrassing questions as to whether the church still possessed those things which in the beginning certified its divinity.[163]

(40) Where no rhetorical cunning could bridge the gap between the views of the fourth century and those of the early church, the latter were frankly discounted as suitable to a state of immaturity beyond which the church had happily progressed, emancipated from the "childish tales and vaporings of old grandmothers."[164] The learned fathers of the fourth and

fifth centuries boast that the wise and noble who shunned the primitive church are now safe in a bosom of a Christian society which preaches and practices things that would have frightened off the rude converts of an earlier day,[165] and invoke the eloquence of Demosthenes against the *simplicitatem rusticam* of the literal minded.[166] This has been the official line ever since, and modern churchmen duly shudder at the thought of being "at the mercy of the primitive Church, *its* teachings, *its* life, *its* understanding,"[167] and congratulate themselves on having outgrown the "fond imaginings of the Apostles."[168]

The Dilemma

Ever since the recent "rediscovery of the importance of eschatology within the New Testament,"[169] scholars have been faced, we are told, with a choice between eschatology and history—*tertium non datur* (there is no third choice).[170] Actually there has always been a third choice, namely to accept the passing of the church as the fulfillment of prophecy in history. But that, of course, is exactly what church history will not allow: "Modern New Testament critics," writes Grant, "insist on the priority of the Church to its written records."[171] The church must be rescued at all price. For that reason it has been necessary to ignore Jeremias's simple and obvious solution to the "vollendeter Widerspruch" (complete contradiction) between the conflicting missionary policies of the early church: the limited preaching belongs to one act of the play, the world preaching to another.[172] This is a thing that Christians will not concede, for if the church is to remain on the scene, the drama must be one act or none.[173]

To preserve this hypothetical unity students have ascribed to the first Christians a fantastic one-package view of the future in which all the culminating events of prophecy are fulfilled at a single stupendous blow, "gathering up into one great climax the many judgments the . . . prophets had foretold."[174] When the great event failed to transpire, the great delay turned the great expectation into the great fiasco (the terms are not ours!), the church passing through the great disappointment to the real fulfillment, the great triumphal procession of the kingdom through the world. Such an unflattering view of the founders' foresight is forced on the experts by a constitutional inability to think of the church as anything but a permanent and growing institution.[175] It was this very attitude, it will be recalled, toward his own church that made it impossible for Trypho the Jew to accept Justin's complicated Messianic history.

But though the "great misunderstanding" theory has the merit of preserving the integrity of the church, it gravely jeopardizes the integrity of its founders while failing to give due consideration to certain peculiar and significant facts, namely, that the early Christians did *not* predict an immediate culmination of everything, but viewed the future down a long vista of prophetic events having more than one "end";[176] that not a single verse of scripture calls for an immediate parousia *or* end of the world;[177] that there is a notable lack of evidence for any early Christian disappointment or surprise at the failure of the parousia.[178] While the enemies of the church exploited every absurdity and inconsistency in its position and made merry over "Jesus the King who never ruled," they never played up what should have been the biggest joke of all—the feverish, hourly expectation of the Lord who never came. For Robert Eisler this strange silence is nothing less than "the most astonishing of all historical paradoxes."[179] But what makes it such is only the refusal of the evidence to match the conventional pattern of church history: if there are no signs whatever of blasted hopes and expectations, we can only conclude that there were no such expectations. There *were* indeed Christians who looked for an immediate coming of the Lord and asked, "Where are the signs of his coming?" but they are expressly branded by the early leaders as false Christians, just as the virgins who expected the quick return of the Master, who "delayed his coming," were the foolish ones.[180]

Students of church history have long been taught that whereas the primitive saints, living in an atmosphere of feverish expectation, looked forward momentarily to the end of everything, the later Christians gradually sobered up and learned to be more realistic. Exactly the opposite was the case, for while there is no evidence that the sober first Christians thought the end of the world was at hand, there is hardly a later theologian who does not think so: "From the days of the early church, through the vicissitudes of the lengthening middle centuries, into the twilight of the medieval day, the conviction of the world's end . . . was part and parcel of Christian thought."[181] It had to be the end of the world, because the end of the church was inadmissible. Yet such was not the case with the first Christians, thoroughly at home with the idea that divine things, while they are preexistent and eternal, are taken away from the earth and restored again from time to time.[182] If the church comes and goes like the moon, it is only with reference to this temporal world where all things are necessarily temporary.[183] A great deal of attention has been given in recent years to early Christian and Jewish concepts of time and history. The present tendency is to treat the church as existing *"sub specie aeternitatis,* et pourtant dans le temps" (*sub specie aeternitatis,* and yet in time) as a supernatural and eschatological entity, "eine Schöpfung von oben her" (a creation from above).[184] This releases it from earthly bonds, as does Ambrose's declaration that the *civitas,* "which lives forever, because it cannot die," desires only to leave the earth in all possible haste and be caught up, literally as Elijah was, into heaven.[185]

To escape the dark interval between the apostles and the parousia, scholars have bored two exits. The one recognizes a catastrophe ahead but postpones it to a vague and distant future,[186] while the other admits that it was near at hand but insists that the damage was not so bad after all.[187] Thus both convictions of the early church, that the end was *near* and that it was to be *disastrous*, receive reluctant confirmation—for no one suggests that only a distant *and* partial disruption was expected. There is a third escape hatch, around which there has been much milling and crowding in recent years, but it seems to be only a false door, a semantic exercise in which the conflicting claims of eschatology and history are simply placed side by side and declared reconciled in various ingenious and symbolic ways. If this vast literature of double-talk, "bewildering in its variety,"[188] shows any perceptible trend, it is an inclination to have eschatology, since it can no longer be brushed aside, swallowed alive by the church: "The Church is an 'eschatological community,' since she is the New Testament, the ultimate and final. . . . The doctrine of Christ finds its fulness and completion in the doctrine of the Church, i.e. of 'the Whole Christ.'"[189] Such language actually seeks to de-eschatologize eschatology by making "mythical and timeless what they [the early Christians] regarded to be real and temporal."[190]

More to the point is the searching question of Schoeps with which we began this survey, whether after all the real church may not have been left behind in the march of history: "Waren sie am Ende doch die wahren Erben, auch wenn sie untergingen?" (At the end were they the real heirs, even if they perished?)[191] We have indicated above some of the reasons for suggesting that the church, like its founder, his apostles, and the prophets before them, came into the world, did the works of the Father, *and then went out of the world,* albeit with a promise of return. Some aspects of the problem, at least, deserve closer attention than students have hitherto been willing to give them.

Notes

1. Karl Bihlmeyer, *Kirchengeschichte* (Paderborn: Schönigh, 1951), part 1:1–2.

2. "There is always danger of a metaphor once adopted becoming the master instead of the servant," writes E. A. Payne, commenting on K. S. Latourette's "Unquenchable Light" in "The Modern Expansion of the Church: Some Reflections on Dr. Latourette's Conclusions," *Journal of Theological Studies* 47 (1946): 151.

3. While suspecting the worst, the fathers could not bring themselves to admit it, according to John Kaye, *Ecclesiastical History of the Second and Third Centuries, Illustrated from the Writings of Tertullian* (London: Farran, 1894), 48–51. See note 139 below.

4. The tension is discussed by René Marlé, "Le Christ de la foi et le Jésus de l'histoire," *Études* 302 (1959): 67–76. Cf. Robert M. Grant, "The Appeal to the Early Fathers," *Journal of Theological Studies*, n.s. 11 (1960): 14, 23.

5. Arnobius, *Adversus gentes (Against the Heathen)* 2.76 (PL 5:934A); 2 Corinthians 4:8–18; Tertullian, *Ad Scapulam (To Scapula)* 1 (PL 1:775–80); Cyprian, *Epistolae (Letters)* 56 (PL 4:362).

6. Matthew 17:12; 21:37–39; 23:31–37; Mark 12:6–8; Luke 17:25; John 1:5, 10–11; 3:11–12, 19, 32; 5:38, 40–47; 7:7; 8:19, 23–24, 37–38, 40–47; 15:22–25; cf. Acts 3:13–15.

7. Matthew 9:15; Luke 9:41; 13:25–27; 17:22; John 12:33–36; 13:33; 14:30; 16:16; cf. Acts 3:21.

8. John 9:4–5; 14:30. Evil triumphs from Abel to the *eschaton:* Matthew 23:35–39; 17:12; Luke 11:51; *Recognitiones Clementinae (Clementine Recognitions)* 3.61 (PG 1:1208).

9. Matthew 10:24–25; Mark 13:13; Luke 10:16; John 15:18–21; 17:14; Acts 28:26–27; Frederick C. Grant, "The Mission of the Disciples," *Journal of Biblical Literature* 35 (1916): 293–314.

10. Matthew 10:16–22, 28; 24:9; Mark 3:9; Luke 10:3; John 16:1, 2, 33; 1 Corinthians 4:9; Clement, *Epistola I ad Corinthios (First Epistle to the Corinthians)* 5 (PG 1:217–20).

11. Matthew 24:14; 28:20; Mark 13:10. See notes 17 and 21 below.

12. James 5:10–11; 1 Peter 1:6–7, 24; 4:12–14; Romans 8:3–17.

13. 1 John 3:1; 1 Peter 5:1; John 17:25.

14. Matthew 16:24–26; Luke 12:22–34; 2 Corinthians 4:8–16; Philippians 3:1–21.

15. Matthew 13:13–30; Romans 1:16–32; 2 Corinthians 11:3–4; 2 Thessalonians 2:7–12; 1 Timothy 4:1–3; 6:20–21; 2 Timothy 4:3–4; 2 Peter 2:1–22; Jude 1:4–11, 16–19.

16. It ends only with the second coming: Matthew 13:30, 39–43; Mark 12:9; 2 Thessalonians 2:8; *Didache* 16; Justin Martyr, *Dialogus cum Tryphone (Dialogue with Trypho)* 51.2 (PG 6:588–89).

17. John 17:25; 1 Peter 5:8; 1 John 3:1.

18. John 14:30; Matthew 21:38; Mark 12:7; Luke 20:14.

19. Matthew 13:24–30, 38. Both *syllegein* and *synagogein* are used.

20. 2 Timothy 4:2–4; 2 Thessalonians 2:9–12; Romans 1:21–31.

21. Matthew 24:14; cf. 10:23; 28:20, where *aeon* refers to that particular age. Oscar Cullmann, "Eschatology and Missions in the New Testament," in *The Background of the New Testament and Its Eschatology*, ed. William D. Davies and David Daube (Cambridge: Cambridge University Press, 1956), 417; cf. Niels W. Messel, *Die Einheitlichkeit der jüdischen Eschatologie* (Giessen: Töpelmann, 1915), 61–69, 44–50. See note 182 below.

22. Mark 13:9–10; Acts 2:16–17, 33; Origen, *Commentaria in Evangelium secundum Matthaeum (Commentary on Matthew)* 39

(PG 13:1655B), concludes that, strictly speaking, *jam finem venisse;* so also Chrysostom, *In Epistolam ad Hebraeos (On the Epistle to the Hebrews)* 21.3 (PG 63:152).

23. Tertullian, *Adversus gnosticos Scorpiace (Scorpiace)* 9–10 (PL 2:162–67); 13–15 (PL 2:171–75); Ignatius, *Epistola ad Polycarpum (Epistle to Polycarp)* 3 (PL 5:709); Ignatius, *Epistola ad Ephesios (Epistle to the Ephesians)* 9 (PL 5:652).

24. Hebrews 6:11; Philippians 3:8–10; 1 Peter 1:4–6, 9; Clement, *Epistola II ad Corinthios (Second Epistle to the Corinthians)* 5.2–4 (PG 1:336); Barnabas, *Epistola catholica (Catholic Epistle)* 8.6 (PG 2:748); Justin, *Apologia pro Christianis (Apology)* 1.57 (PG 6:413–16).

25. Mark 13:34–37; 1 Peter 4:12–13. Like soldiers, each is to remain at his post. Clement, *First Epistle to the Corinthians* 37 (PG 1:281–84); 21 (PG 1:256); Tertullian, *Liber ad martyres (To the Martyrs)* 3 (PL 1:707–9); cf. Clement, *First Epistle to the Corinthians* 5 (PG 1:217–20); Ignatius, *Epistle to Polycarp* 3 (PL 5:709–10); Ignatius, *Epistola ad Magnesios (Epistle to the Magnesians)* 5 (PG 5:761–64); Barnabas, *Catholic Epistle* 2.1 (PG 2:729–30).

26. "Ita ut pauci remaneant certantes pro veritate usque ad finem, qui et salvandi sunt soli." Origen, *Commentary on Matthew* 24 (PG 13:1654D). There were few martyrs, G. de Ste. Croix, "Aspects of the 'Great' Persecution," *Harvard Theological Review* 47 (1954): 104, and countless betrayers, W. H. Frend, "Failure of the Persecutions in the Roman Empire," *Past and Present* 16 (November 1959): 15–16.

27. Early sources speak of two factions within the church and of the "seducers" completely exterminating the righteous party. Carl Schmidt, *Gespräche Jesu mit seinen Jüngern nach der Auferstehung* (Leipzig: Hinrichs, 1919); cf. Samuel G. F. Brandon, *The Fall of Jerusalem and the Christian Church* (London: Society for the Promotion of Christian Knowledge, 1951), 54.

28. Luke 13:25–30; Matthew 23:29. There is a time limit to the promise, Hebrews 12:17, and "when the tower is finished, you will

wish to do good, and will have no opportunity." Shepherd of Hermas, *Visio (Visions)* 3.9 (PG 2:907).

29. Justin, *Dialogue with Trypho* 110 (PG 6:729); Hilary, *Contra Constantium Imperatorem (Against the Emperor Constantius)* 4 (PL 10:581B).

30. Galatians 3:1–4. Ignatius describes the corruption with striking imagery as of pleasing and plausible wolves. *Epistola ad Philadelphenses (Epistle to the Philadelphians)* 2 (PG 5:697–708); a goodly label on a bottle of poison, a deadly drug mixed with sweet wine, *Epistola ad Trallianos (Epistle to the Trallians)* 6 (PG 5: 679–80); a counterfeit coin, *Epistle to the Magnesians* 5 (PG 5:647–48); cleverly baited hooks, *Epistle to the Magnesians* 11 (PG 5:653–56), etc.

31. Rudolf Bultmann, "History and Eschatology in the New Testament," *New Testament Studies* 1 (1954): 7–8.

32. A mixture of "Freude, Sehnsucht, und bange Furcht." Rudolf Knopf, *Die Zukunftshoffnungen des Urchristentums* (Tübingen: Mohr, 1907), 7–11. Cf. *Didache* 16.

33. Clement, *First Epistle to the Corinthians* 41.4 (PG 1: 289–92). "The last stumbling-block approaches." Barnabas, *Catholic Epistle* 4.3 and 9 (PG 2:731–34); Clement, *First Epistle to the Corinthians* 7.1 (PG 1:221–25); Clement, *Second Epistle to the Corinthians* 7–8 (PG 1:337–41); Shepherd of Hermas, *Visions* 2.2 (PG 2:897); 4.1 (PG 2:909).

34. Clement, *First Epistle to the Corinthians* 15.4–6 (PG 1:237–40); 8 (PG 1:225–28); 39 (PG 1:285–88); 57 (PG 1:324–26); Clement, *Second Epistle to the Corinthians* 6 (PG 1:336–37); Barnabas, *Catholic Epistle* 4–5 (PG 2:731–37); 13–14 (PG 2:765–69).

35. Clement, *First Epistle to the Corinthians* 57–58 (PG 1:324–28). The promise of the Paraclete is no guarantee. Clement, *Second Epistle to the Corinthians* 6.9 (PG 1:336–37).

36. So Clement, *First Epistle to the Corinthians* 3–7 (PG 1:213–25); Barnabas, *Catholic Epistle* 2–6 (PG 2:729–44); 16 (PG 2:773–76);

Constitutiones apostolicae (Apostolic Constitutions) 7.32 (PG 1:1621); Lactantius, *Divinae institutiones (Divine Institutes)* 7.17 (PL 6:1008–9).

37. Clement, *First Epistle to the Corinthians* 1 (PG 1:201); 3 (PG 1:213); 19 (PG 1:248); 41 (PG 1:289); 47 (PG 1:305–8); 52 (PG 1:316); Barnabas, *Catholic Epistle* 2 (PG 2:729); Ignatius, *Epistle to the Ephesians* 17 (PG 5:749–52); Ignatius, *Epistle to the Phila-delphians* 2 (PG 5:820); Shepherd of Hermas, *Visions* 2.2 (PG 2:897); 3.9 (PG 2:907); Shepherd of Hermas, *Similitudo (Similitudes)* 7 (PG 2:969–72); 9.21 and 25–26 (PG 2:999–1002); 10.1 (PG 2:1009).

38. *Didache* 10.5; Ignatius, *Epistle to Polycarp* 1.2 (PG 5:861–64); Ignatius, *Epistle to the Ephesians* 17 (PG 5:749–52); Ignatius, *Epistle to the Philadelphians* 1 (PG 5:820); Shepherd of Hermas, *Similitudes* 9.14 (PG 2:917); Barnabas, *Catholic Epistle* 2.1 (PG 2:729); 21 (PG 2:779–81).

39. Clement, *First Epistle to the Corinthians* 15 (PG 1:237); 30 (PG 1:269–72); Clement, *Second Epistle to the Corinthians* 3–4 (PG 1:333–36); Barnabas, *Catholic Epistle* 10.4 (PG 2:752–56); Ignatius, *Epistle to the Ephesians* 15 (PG 5:657); 7 (PG 5:649); Ignatius, *Epistle to the Magnesians* 4 (PG 5:648); Ignatius, *Epistle to the Trallians* 6 (PG 5:680); Polycarp, *Epistola ad Philippenses (Epistle to the Philippians)* 10 (PG 5:1013); Shepherd of Hermas, *Visions* 1.3 (PG 2:893–96); Shepherd of Hermas, *Similitudes* 9.13 (PG 2:991); 9.21 (PG 2:999).

40. Polycarp, *Epistle to the Philippians* 7 (PG 5:1012); Shepherd of Hermas, *Mandatum (Mandates)* 11.1 (PG 2:943).

41. Ignatius, *Epistle to the Magnesians* 5 (PG 5:648); Clement, *Second Epistle to the Corinthians* 6 (PG 1:336–37); Barnabas, *Catholic Epistle* 5 (PG 2:733); 18 (PG 2:776); see Kirsopp Lake's note on the Shepherd of Hermas in his translation of *Apostolic Fathers,* LCL (Cambridge: Harvard University Press, 1912), 2:21 n. 1.

42. Clement, *First Epistle to the Corinthians* 1 (PG 1:201–8); 3 (PG 1:213–16); 19 (PG 1:248); 24 (PG 1:260–61); Ignatius, *Epistle to the Trallians* 7 (PG 5:764–65); Ignatius, *Epistle to the Ephesians* 9.5

(PG 5:713); 17 (PG 5:749–52); Shepherd of Hermas, *Visions* 3.3 (PG 2:901); 10 (PG 2:907). Cf. *Testament of Hezekiah* 2:3B–4:18 (*OTP* 2:159–61).

43. Barnabas, *Catholic Epistle* 16 (PG 2:771–76); *Didache* 16.3; Enoch 89; 56; 66–67; Logion 14, in "Prétendues sentences de Jésus" (PO 4:176–77); cf. "Le Salut—les vieux sages" (PO 9:227–28).

44. Shepherd of Hermas, *Visions* 3.3–7 (PG 2:901–6).

45. Ibid., 3.11–13 (PG 2:907–10).

46. Shepherd of Hermas, *Similitudes* 3 (PG 2:955); 4 (PG 2:955–58); 9 (PG 2:979–1010); Clement, *First Epistle to the Corinthians* 58 (PG 5:328); Eusebius, *Historia ecclesiastica (Ecclesiastical History)* 3.31.3 (PG 20:280–81); 5.24.2 (PG 20:493–508).

47. A. D. Nock, "The Vocabulary of the New Testament," *Journal of Biblical Literature* 52 (1933): 135.

48. Hilary, *Liber contra Auxentium (Against Auxentius)* 4 (PL 10:611B).

49. K. Holl, "Urchristentum und Religionsgeschichte," *Zeitschrift für systematische Theologie* 2 (1924): 403–5; Suzanne de Dietrich, *Le Dessein de Dieu*, 2nd ed. (Neuchâtel: Delachaux and Niestlé, 1948), 19, finds only one case, Mark 5:19, in which Christ did not avoid publicity.

50. Origen, *Contra Celsum (Against Celsus)* 2.76 (PG 11:848); 4.28 (PG 11:1068); Minucius Felix, *Octavius* 7–11 (PL 3:262–81); Lactantius, *Divine Institutes* 5.7 (PL 6:991).

51. Minucius Felix, *Octavius* 9–10 (PL 3:270–76); Justin, *Dialogue with Trypho* 52 (PG 6:589–92—the parousia a secret); 90.2 (PG 6:689–92); Tertullian, *Apologeticus adversus Gentes pro Christianis (Apology)* 7 (PL 1:358–62); *Clementine Recognitions* 1.52 (PG 1:1236); Clement of Alexandria, *Stromata* 1.12 (PG 8:753); 5.10 (PG 9:93–101).

52. Matthew 13:9–17; *Clementine Recognitions* 2.60 (PG 1:1264); 3.1 (PG 1:1281–82); Tertullian, *De praescriptionibus (The Prescription against Heretics)* 25–26 (PL 2:43–46); Origen, *Against Celsus* 1.1.1–7 (PG 11:651–69); Ignatius, *Epistle to the Trallians* 5 (PG 5:781–84).

53. Origen, *Peri archōn (On First Things)* 1.2 (PG 11:130–45); 1.4 (PG 11:155); 1.6–8 (PG 11:165–83).

54. Origen, *Against Celsus* 2.70 (PG 11:905–8); Albert Schweitzer, *Geschichte der Leben-Jesu-Forschung* (Tübingen: Mohr, 1951), 396. This is an edition of the earlier *Von Reimarus zu Wrede;* cf. English translation, *The Quest of the Historical Jesus* (New York: Macmillan, 1961). Herman Gunkel, *Zum religionsgeschichtlichen Verständnis des Neuen Testaments* (Göttingen: Vandenhoeck and Ruprecht, 1903), 78–79; Kirsopp Lake, *Introduction to the New Testament* (New York: Harper, 1937), 37.

55. Irenaeus, *Contra haereses (Against Heresies)* 4.33.7 (PG 7:1076–77); 2.27.1–3 (PG 7:802), insists that nothing has been lost—cf. 1.8.1 (PG 7:519, etc.)—yet speaks with awe of the knowledge of the apostles, 1.13.6 (PG 7:588); 3.2.2 (PG 7:847), which Ignatius implies far exceeds his own, *Epistle to the Ephesians* 3 (PG 5:645); *Epistle to the Magnesians* 5 (PG 5:648); *Epistola ad Romanos (Epistle to the Romans)* 4 (PG 5:689). Later fathers were intrigued by the great unwritten knowledge of the apostles. Gottfried Thomasius, *Die Dogmengeschichte der alten Kirche* (Erlangen: Deichert, 1886), 209, 297–98.

56. Joachim Jeremias, *Jesu Verheissung für die Völker* (Stuttgart: Kohlhammer, 1956), 15–16, 61–62 = *Jesus' Promise to the Nations,* trans. S. H. Hooke (London: SCM Press, 1958).

57. Albert Dufourcq, *Epoque syncrétiste: Histoire de la fondation de l'église, la révolution religieuse* (Paris: Blond, 1909), 220; Jeremias, *Jesu Verheissung für die Völker,* 17, 21, 60–61. See note 38 above.

58. *Didache* 10.5; Ignatius, *Epistle to the Romans* 7 (PG 5:693): "deuro pros ton patera"—literally.

59. Discussed by Olof Linton, *Das Problem der Urkirche in der neueren Forschung* (Uppsala: Almquist and Wiksell, 1932), 198–200.

60. Robert Eisler, *Iesous basileus ou basileusas* (Heidelberg: Winter, 1930), 2:237.

61. Brandon, *Fall of Jerusalem,* 7–11.

62. *Homiliae Clementinae (Clementine Homilies)* 11.16.21 (PG 2:384A); Hippolytus, *De consummatione mundi* (spuria) *(On the Consummation of the World)* 10–11 (PG 10:913A–C); Athanasius, *Vita Antonii (Life of Antony)* 82 (PG 26:957).

63. *Acta Pilati (Acts of Pilate)* 15 (PO 9:108–9); James R. Harris, *Gospel of the Twelve Apostles* (Cambridge: Cambridge University Press, 1900), 28, 33, 35, 38; E. A. Wallis Budge, *Contendings of the Apostles* (London: Oxford University Press, 1899–1901), 2:62, 53–55, 59.

64. Lake, *Introduction to the New Testament,* 62.

65. Robert M. Grant, *Second Century Christianity* (London: Society for Promoting Christian Knowledge, 1946), 9.

66. Eusebius, *Ecclesiastical History* 3.32.7–8 (PG 20:281–84).

67. Robert L. P. Milburn, *Early Christian Interpretations of History* (London: Black, 1954), 25–26.

68. Gustave Bardy, "L'église et son enseignement pendant les trois premiers siècles," *Revue des sciences religieuses* 12 (1932): 1, quoting Tertullian, *Apology* 18.4 (PL 1:362–65).

69. Eugéne de Faye, *Étude sur les origines des églises de l'âge apostolique* (Paris: Leroux, 1909), 111.

70. For example, Shepherd of Hermas, *Visions* 1.3 (PG 2:891–93); 2.2 (PG 2:895–97); 3.9 (PG 2:897); Shepherd of Hermas, *Similitudes* 9.19 (PG 2:997); Shepherd of Hermas, *Mandates* 11–12 (PG 2:943); Clement, *First Epistle to the Corinthians* 21 (PG 1:256). Cf. Eusebius, *Ecclesiastical History* 5.28 (PG 20:512); *Clementine Recognitions* 1.1–5 (PG 1:1207–9).

71. See Marlé, "Christ de la foi," 67–76.

72. Origen, *Against Celsus* 8.72 and 8.74 (PG 11:1624–29); Tertullian, *Apology* 38 (PL 1:526–31); *Apostolic Constitutions* 7.39 (PG 1:1037–40); Barnabas, *Catholic Epistle* 2 (PG 2:729); 4 (PG 2:731); 1 Corinthians 7:29–32.

73. Origen, *Against Celsus* 8.17–20 (PG 11:1540–49); Zeno, *Liber (Commentary)* 1, *Tractatus (Tractate)* 14 (PL 11:354B–358A); Minucius

Felix, *Octavius* 10 (PL 3:274); Jerome, *Epistolae (Letters)* 130.15 (PL 22:1119A); Arnobius, *Against the Heathen* 6.1 (PL 5:1162B).

74. Shepherd of Hermas, *Similitudes* 1.1 (PG 2:951); Clement, *Second Epistle to the Corinthians* 5 (PG 1:336); Cyprian, *Liber de mortalitate (Treatise on Mortality)* 25 (PL 4:623B).

75. Hans Lietzmann, *Geschichte der alten Kirche* (Berlin: de Gruyter, 1932–34), 2:41–42 = *The Founding of the Church Universal,* trans. Bertram L. Woolf, 2nd ed. (London: Nicholson and Watson, 1950); Ernst Käsemann, *Das wandernde Gottesvolk* (Göttingen: Vandenhoeck and Ruprecht, 1939), 51–52.

76. Tertullian, *The Prescription against Heretics* 27–29 (PL 2:46–48); Polycarp, *Epistle to the Philippians* 9 (PG 5:1012–13).

77. Acts 17:6; 2 Timothy 4:6–8. Conversion not the object, 1 Corinthians 1:17.

78. Cullmann, "Eschatology and Missions," 415.

79. 1 Corinthians 9:16; John 15:22; Matthew 23:34–35; 27:25; Luke 11:49–51; Acts 5:28; 18:6; *Clementine Recognitions* 1.8 (PG 1:1211): "tacere non possumus."

80. Oscar Cullmann, *Urchristentum und Gottesdienst* (Zürich: Zwingli, 1950), 39–56.

81. Ignatius, *Epistle to the Romans* 6–8 (PG 5:691–94); Ignatius, *Epistle to the Ephesians* 11.1 (PG 5:654); *Passio s. Perpetuae* 6; 18; 21. Quotation from *Apostolic Constitutions* 5.5 (PG 1:833).

82. Eusebius, *Ecclesiastical History* 6.45 (PG 20:633).

83. Tertullian, *Apology* 1 (PL 1:305–8); Cyprian, *Treatise on Mortality* 12 (PL 4:611–12).

84. Eduard Norden, *Die antike Kunstprosa* (Leipzig: Teubner, 1898) 2:418–19, contrasts the early and later Christian concepts of martyrdom. The transition is clear in Cyprian, who must warn, "non martyres Evangelium faciant." *Letters* 24 (22) (PL 4:293A).

85. Cyprian, *Letters* 8 (PL 4:255A); Cyprian, *De duplici martyrio (On the Twofold Martyrdom)* 35 (PL 4:982A); Clement of Alexandria, *Stromata* 4.7 (PG 8:1268–80); Leo, *Sermo* 47.1 (PL 54:295B–C).

86. So Asterius Urbanus, *Fragmenta contra Montanistas (Against the Montanists)* frg. 3; 6; 8 (PG 10:149B, 153A–B).

87. So Optatus, *De schismate Donatistarum (On the Donatist Schism)* 17, 24–26 (PL 11:968–69, 979B–986A).

88. Cyprian, *Epistola ad Fortunatum (Letter to Fortunatus)* Praefatio (PL 4:678–82).

89. Clarence T. Craig, *The Beginnings of Christianity* (New York: Abingdon-Cokesbury, 1943), 328.

90. Pieter A. van Stempvoort, "Het onstaan van het Kerkbegrip en de oudste Kerkorganisatie," in *Het Oudste Christendom en de antieke Cultuur,* ed. J. H. Waszink et al. (Haarlem: Tjeenk Willink, 1951), 2:331; Brandon, *Fall of Jerusalem,* 9–11. The imagery goes back to Eusebius, *Ecclesiastical History* 1.1.3 (PG 20:48–53).

91. Brandon, *Fall of Jerusalem,* 10; Eduard Schwartz, *Kaiser Constantin und die christliche Kirche* (Leipzig: Teubner, 1913), 17–18; Hans Lietzmann, *Kleine Schriften* (Berlin: Akademie-Verlag, 1958–62), 1:97.

92. Theodore Brandt, *Die Kirche im Wandel der Zeit* (Leipzig: MBK-Verlag, 1933), 79.

93. E. C. Blackman, "The Task of Exegesis," in Davies and Daube, *Background of the New Testament,* 13.

94. Gustave Bardy, *La conversion au christianisme* (Paris: Aubier, 1949), 296.

95. Dufourcq, *Epoque syncrétiste,* 250; Maurice Goguel, *Les premiers temps de l'église* (Neuchâtel: Delachaux and Niestlé, 1949), 139; and Maurice Goguel, "La seconde génération chrétienne," *Revue de l'histoire des religions* 136 (1949): 36–37.

96. Eusebius, *Ecclesiastical History* 3.37 (PG 20:292–93); 3.39 (PG 20:292–302); Clement, *First Epistle to the Corinthians* 47 (PG 1:305–8); Polycarp, *Epistle to the Philippians* 3 (PG 5:1008); Ignatius, *Epistle to the Romans* 5 (PG 5:809–12); Irenaeus, *Against Heresies* 3.3.4 (PG 7:851); Methodius, *Ex libro de resurrectione (From the Treatise on Resurrection)* 6 (PG 18:313B).

97. Eusebius, *Ecclesiastical History* 3.39.1–4 (PG 20:297); 5.10.4 (PG 20:453–56); 11.3–5 (PG 20:456–57); Justin, *Dialogue with Trypho* 82 (PG 6:669–72); Origen, *Against Celsus* 2.8 (PG 11:805–8).

98. Eusebius, *Ecclesiastical History* 3.32.7–8 (PG 20:281–86); 2.1.3 (PG 20:140–41); Irenaeus, *Against Heresies* 1 (PG 7:437–45).

99. Polycarp, *Epistle to the Philippians* 3 (PG 5:1008); Barnabas, *Catholic Epistle* 1.5 (PG 2:727); the case of Ignatius is discussed by Jean Réville, "Études sur les origines de l'épiscopat," *Revue de l'histoire religieuse* 22 (1890): 285–88.

100. D. Busy, "L'adversaire et l'obstacle (2 Thess. 2:3–12)," *Recherches de science religieuse* 24 (1934): 431.

101. Bardy, *Conversion au christianisme*, 306; Grant, *Second Century Christianity*, 9–18.

102. "Singuli quique coetus haereticorum se potissimum Christianos, et suam esse Catholicam Ecclesiam putant." Lactantius, *Divine Institutes* 4.30 (PL 6:540–44); Eusebius, *Ecclesiastical History* 5.13–18 (PG 20:460–81); Sozomen, *Historia Ecclesiastica (Ecclesiastical History)* 5.9 (PG 67:1237–40); 5.20 (PG 67:1277–80); 6.26 (PG 67:1361–66); 8.20 (PG 67:1568–70), etc. Origen, *Against Celsus* 3.10–12 (PG 11:932–36).

103. Justin, *Apology* 8 (PG 6:338–40); Justin, *Dialogue with Trypho* 35 (PG 6:549–53); 42 (PG 6:565); 80 (PG 6:664–80); cf. Origen, *Against Celsus* 6.11 (PG 11:1305–8).

104. Eusebius, *Ecclesiastical History* 5.16 (PG 20:464–72); Justin, *Quaestiones (Inquiries)* nos. 5 and 100 (PG 6:1256AB, 1344–45).

105. Sulpicius Severus, *Historia sacra (Sacred History)* 2.46 (PL 20:155); 2.50 (PL 20:157–58). Eusebius worried too. Walther Völker, "Von welchen Tendenzen liess sich Eusebius bei Abfassung seiner 'Kirchengeschichte' Leiten?" *Vigiliae christianae* 4 (1950): 170–71.

106. Adolf von Harnack, *Lehrbuch der Dogmengeschichte*, 5th ed. (Tübingen: Mohr, 1931), 1:250; Eusebius, *Ecclesiastical History* 5.15–16 (PG 20:172–73).

107. The Reformation itself attempted revival of "prophetic, eschatological Christianity." Heinrich Bornkamm, *Grundriss zum Studium der Kirchengeschichte* (Gütersloh: Bertelsmann, 1949), 63.

108. Adolf von Harnack, *Das Mönchtum* (Giessen: Ricken, 1895), passim. The church fathers did not encourage pilgrimages. Bernard Kötting, *Peregrinatio Religiosa* (Münster: Regensberg, 1950), 421.

109. Goguel, *Les premiers temps de l'église,* 34, 180, 192–94.

110. Bardy, *Conversion au christianisme,* 304; so Lietzmann, *Geschichte der alten Kirche,* 1:226; Harnack, *Das Mönchtum,* 25.

111. Robert Frick, *Die Geschichte des Reich-Gottes-Gedankens in der alten Kirche bis zu Origenes und Augustin,* supplement 6 of Zeitschrift für die neutestamentliche Wissenschaft (Giessen: Töpelmann, 1928), 154; Goguel, *Les premiers temps de l'église,* 35; Harnack, *Das Mönchtum,* 25.

112. Bultmann, "History and Eschatology in the New Testament," 15.

113. Goguel, *Les premiers temps de l'église,* 191.

114. Milburn, *Early Christian Interpretations of History,* 26.

115. Gustave Bardy, *L'Église et les derniers Romains* (Paris: Laffont, 1948), 48.

116. F.-M. Braun, "Où en est l'eschatologie du Nouveau Testament," *Revue biblique* 49 (1940): 53; Henri Leclercq, "Églises," in *Dictionnaire d'archéologie chrétienne et de liturgie,* ed. Fernand Cabrol and Henri Leclerq (Paris: Letouzey et Ané, 1907–53), 4:2281.

117. Johannes de Zwaan, "Some Remarks on the 'Church Idea' in the Second Century," in *Aux sources de la tradition chrétienne: Mélanges offerts à M. Maurice Goguel* (Neuchâtel: Delachaux and Niestlé, 1950), 278.

118. Tertullian, *De pudicitia (On Modesty)* 21 (PL 2:1080B).

119. Bultmann, "History and Eschatology in the New Testament," 15.

120. Wilhelm von Christ, *Geschichte der griechischen Literatur,* 6th ed. (Munich: Beck, 1924), 955.

121. "In the end therefore, it was the Christian doctrine and practice which underwent the change, and society which remained." Kirsopp Lake, "The Shepherd of Hermas and Christian Life in Rome in the Second Century," *Harvard Theological Review* 4 (1911): 25.

122. Louis M. O. Duchesne, *Origenes du culte chrétien,* 2nd ed. (Paris: Thorin, 1898), 52–53; 5th ed. (1920), 55.

123. Lake, *Introduction to the New Testament,* 22; Dufourcq, *Epoque syncrétiste,* 221.

124. Goguel, *Les premiers temps de l'église,* 209; Reinhold Seeberg, *Textbook of the History of Doctrines* (Grand Rapids: Baker Book House, 1952), 1:118; Karl Adam, *Das Wesen des Katholizismus* (Düsseldorf: Schwann, 1934), 194 = *The Spirit of Catholicism,* trans. Justin McCann (London: Sheed and Ward, 1929).

125. Norden, *Die antike Kunstprosa,* 2:479–81.

126. Linton, *Das Problem der Urkirche,* 160, 164–66; Otto Kuss, "Zur Senfkornparabel," *Theologie und Glaube* 41 (1951): 40–46; Jeremias, *Jesu Verheissung für die Völker,* 58–59; cf. English ed., 68–69.

127. So Bardy, *Conversion au christianisme,* 6; Bornkamm, *Grundriss zum Studium der Kirchengeschichte,* 20.

128. Stanley Bonner, *Roman Declamation* (Liverpool: Liverpool University Press, 1949), 59.

129. "Animae emptae a Christo non potuerunt vendi." Optatus, *On the Donatist Schism* 3.11 (PL 11:1024–25); Erich Fascher, "Dynamis Theou," *Zeitschrift für Theologie und Kirche* 19 (1938): 108; Chrysostom exposes the fallacy. *In Epistolam ad Galatas commentarius (Commentary on the Epistle to the Galatians)* 3.2 (PG 61:649–50).

130. Bardy, *Conversion au christianisme,* chap. 8. Refuted by Chrysostom, *On the Epistle to the Hebrews* 5, Homily 8 (PG 63:73), and Salvianus, *De gubernatione Dei (On the Government of God)* 4.1.61.

131. Justin, *Dialogue with Trypho* 35 (PG 6:549–53); Origen, *Against Celsus* 3.12 (PG 11:933–36).

132. Matthew 7:22; 24:5; Mark 9:39; 13:6; Luke 21:8; Acts 17:15.

133. For example, the gloating attacks on the dead Julian. Norden, *Die antike Kunstprosa*, 2:563.

134. Ibid., 2:460–62, 465, 476–77, 529–32, 680–83; Frend, "Failure of the Persecutions," 12.

135. Hippolytus, *Fragmenta in Danielem (Fragments on Daniel)* 5.7 (PG 10:681D); *Demonstratio de Christo et Antichristo (On Christ and the Antichrist)* 29, 57–58 (PG 10:749B, 776B–777A); and *On the Consummation of the World* 11 (PG 10:913C).

136. Hilary, *De Trinitate (On the Trinity)* 10.55 (PL 10:387).

137. Quote is from Chrysostom, *Commentary on Matthew* 46.1 (PG 58:476).

138. Johannes Straub, "Christliche Geschichtesapologetik in der Krisis des römischen Reiches," *Historia* 1 (1950): 64.

139. Basil the Great, *Epistolae (Letters)* 150.2, no. 139 (PG 32:584A). Tertullian, *Prescription against Heretics* 27–28 (PL 2:46–47), must console himself with the argument of numbers. Even before Eusebius, *Praeparatio evangelica (Preparation for the Gospel)* 1.3 (PG 21:33), Hegesippus sought to reassure himself that there was an absolute continuity, according to Louis M. O. Duchesne, *Le Liber Pontificalis* (Paris: Thorin, 1886–92), 1:1, who vainly seeks the same assurance; see Henri Leclercq, "Historiens du Christianisme," in *Dictionnaire d'archéologie chrétienne et de liturgie*, 6:2697.

140. Eusebius, *Ecclesiastical History* 10.4.12–16 (PG 20:857–60); 8.1.8–ii (PG 20:740–44); 8.1–3 (PG 20:744); cf. Sozomen, *Ecclesiastical History* 3.17 (PG 67:1093–96). The church was overcome by its own sins. Cyprian, *Letters* 7 (PL 4:246–51). Cf. *Liber de lapsis (Book on the Apostates)* (PL 4:478–510). On the restoration motif, see Michael S. Seidlmayer, "Rom und Romgedanke im Mittelalter," *Saeculum* 7 (1956): 405–7; John E. Sandys, *History of Classical Scholarship* (New York: Hafner, 1958), 1:513–14.

141. Ambrose, *Hexaemeron* 4.32 (PL 14:217–18); Methodius, *Convivium decem virginum (Banquet of the Ten Virgins)* 6 (PG 18:148B); Jerome, *Commentarius in Isaiah prophetam (Commentary on Isaiah)* 18.66 (PL 24:699–702); Lactantius, *Divine Institutes* 5.7 (PL 6:570–71).

142. Discussed in Hugh W. Nibley, "The Unsolved Loyalty Problem: Our Western Heritage," in *The Ancient State* (Salt Lake City: Deseret Book and FARMS, 1991), 207–12.

143. The surprise is expressed by Chrysostom, *Expositio in Psalmos (Exposition on Psalms)* 148.4 (PG 55:483–84), and *Contra Judaeos et Gentiles, quod Christus sit Deus (Against the Jews and the Gentiles, That Christ Is God)* 12 (PG 48:829–30); cf. the perplexity in Justin, *Inquiries* 74 (PG 6:1316A).

144. Chrysostom, *Sermo antequam iret in exsilium (Discourse before Going into Exile)* 1.2 (PG 52:429–30), and *In illud, vidi Dominum, homilia (Homily on the Verse "I have seen the Lord")* 4.2 (PG 56:121).

145. Völker, "Von welchen Tendenzen," 161–80. J. Burckhardt calls Eusebius "the first thoroughly dishonest historian," cited by Moses Hadas, "The Conversion of Constantine," *Jewish Quarterly Review* 41 (1950): 423.

146. See Nibley, "Unsolved Loyalty Problem," 210–12.

147. Lactantius, *Divine Institutes* 5.24 (PL 6:630).

148. Eusebius, *Commentarius in Lucam (Commentary on Luke)* 27.27 (PG 24:584D–585A).

149. Hilary, *Commentarius in Matthaeum (Commentary on Matthew)* 26.4 (PL 9:1057B).

150. Eusebius, *Commentary on Luke* 13.32 (PG 24:601D–604A).

151. Chrysostom, *De decem millium talentorum debitore homilia (Homily on the Man Who Owed Ten Thousand Talents)* 3 (PG 51:21B).

152. First suggested by Origen, *Commentary on Matthew* 39 (PG 13:1653D).

153. Hilary, *Commentary on Matthew* 25.8 (PL 9:1055).

154. Ibid., 26.6 (PL 9:1058B).

155. Eusebius, *Commentarius in Isaiam prophetam (Commentary on Isaiah)* 11.6 (PG 24:172C–173A).

156. Optatus, *On the Donatist Schism* 7.2 (PL 11:1085B–1086A).

157. A favorite theme with Chrysostom, for example, *Homily on the Verse "I have seen the Lord"* 4.4.2 (PG 56:121); *Sermo post reditum ab exsilio (Discourse following the Return from Exile)* 2 (PG 52:440, 442); *Sermo ipsius severiani de pace (A Sermon on Peace by Severianus Himself)* (PG 52:425); cf. Athanasius II, *Homilia de semente (Homily on the Seed)* 5 (PG 28:149C).

158. Chrysostom, *De novem diebus (On the Nine Days)* 6 (PG 56:277–78); Basil, *Homilia de gratiarum actione (Homily on the Effect of Graces)* 4 (PG 31:228A); Hilary, *On the Trinity* 10.39–43 (PL 10:374–77).

159. Chrysostom, *On the Nine Days* 6 (PG 56:277–78).

160. Edward Gibbon, *Decline and Fall of the Roman Empire* (New York: The Modern Library, 1932), 1:941 n. 101.

161. Chrysostom, *De capto Eutropio et de divitiarum vanitate (On the Capture of Eutropius and the Vanity of Wealth)* 1.6 (PG 52:397–98, 402); *Cum de expulsione ipsius Sancti Joannes ageretur (On the Expulsion of St. John Himself)* (PG 52:433); *Exposition on the Psalms* 147.4 (PG 55:483); *Homily on the Verse "I Have Seen the Lord"* 4.2 (PG 56:121); *Commentary on Matthew* 54.2 (PG 58:535); 77.1 (PG 58:702).

162. Chrysostom, *In Epistolam I ad Corinthios homilia (Homily on the First Epistle to the Corinthians)* 32.1 (PG 61:265); 6.3–4 (PG 61:51–53).

163. Chrysostom, *De sancta Pentecoste homilia (Homily on the Holy Pentecost)* 1.4 (PG 50:459, 453); *De laudibus Sancti Pauli Apostoli homilia (Homilies on the Praise of St. Paul the Apostle)* 4 (PG 50:488); *In inscriptionem Actorum (Inscription on the Acts)* 2.3 (PG 51:81–82; cf. 85); *Homily on the First Epistle to the Corinthians* 32.2 (PG 61:265); *In Colossenses homilia (Homily on Colossians)* 3.8 (PG 62:358–59), etc.

164. Chrysostom, *Exposition on Psalms* 110.4 (PG 55:285); Jerome, *Commentary on Isaiah* 54.1 (PL 24:516B); 13 (PL 24:627B–629A); Origen, *Against Celsus* 4.80 (PG 11:1152–53); Origen, *De principiis (On the First Principles)* 2.4.3 (PG 11:201–3).

165. Athanasius, *Oratio de incarnatione verbi Dei (Oration on the Incarnation of the Word)* 53 (PG 25:189); Jerome, *Letters* 66.4 (PL 22:641); Jerome, *Commentary on Isaiah* 60.1 (PL 24:588D–589A).

166. Jerome, *Contra Joannem Hierosolymitanum (Against John the Jerusalemite)* 11–12 (PL 23:380C–381C).

167. Krister Stendahl, "Implications of Form-Criticism and Tradition-Criticism for Biblical Interpretation," *Journal of Biblical Literature* 77 (1958): 34.

168. A. C. Cotter, "The Eschatological Discourse," *Catholic Biblical Quarterly* 1 (1939): 205.

169. N. A. Dahl, "Christ, Creation, and the Church," in Davies and Daube, *Background of the New Testament,* 422.

170. Schweitzer, *Geschichte der Leben-Jesu-Forschung,* 375.

171. Robert M. Grant, "'Development' in Early Christian Doctrine," *Journal of Religion* 39 (1959): 121.

172. Jeremias, *Jesu Verheissung für die Völker,* 47.

173. So Johannes Weiss, "Das Problem der Entestehung des Christentums," *Archiv für Religionswissenschaft* 16 (1913): 435.

174. Alfred Fawkes, "The Development of Christian Institutions and Beliefs," *Harvard Theological Review* 10 (1917): 115–16.

175. Linton, *Das Problem der Urkirche,* 121, 159.

176. A. Feuillet, "La synthése eschatologique de Saint Matthieu," *Revue biblique* 57 (1950): 180–211; Millar Burrows, *An Outline of Biblical Theology* (Philadelphia: Westminster, 1946), 199–201.

177. Van Stempvoort, "Het ontstaan van het Kerkbegrip," 250; T. F. Glasson, "The Kerygma: Is Our Version Correct," *Hibbert Journal* 51 (1953): 129, 131–32; Frederick A. M. Spencer, "The Second Advent According to the Gospels," *Church Quarterly Review* 126 (1938): 6.

178. Goguel, "La seconde génération chrétienne," 190; G. Born-kamm, *In Memoriam Ernst Lohmeyer* (Stuttgart: Evangelisches Ver-lagswerk, 1951), 116, 118, 121; E. Stauffer, "Agnostos Christos," in Davies and Daube, *Background of the New Testament*, 281–82.

179. Eisler, *Iesous basileus*, 1:26; cf. S. Franck, "Le royaume de dieuonde," *Dieu vivant* 7 (1951): 17–34.

180. Clement, *First Epistle to the Corinthians* 23 (PG 1:236); Clement, *Second Epistle to the Corinthians* 11–12 (PG 2:344–48); Barnabas, *Catholic Epistle* 4.16 (PG 2:731–33); cf. Luke 18:7.

181. R. C. Petry, "Medieval Eschatology and St. Francis of Assisi," *Church History* 9 (1940): 55; Friedrich Bäthgen, *Der Engelpapst* (Halle: Niemeyer, 1933), 76.

182. The old dispensation theory: Origen, *Against Celsus* 4.11–12 (PG 11:1039–41); Milburn, *Early Christian Interpretations of History*, 29–31. The Jews had lost and regained the temple more than once.

183. Epiphanius, *Adversus Haereses (Against Heresies)* 3.2.6 (PG 42:784); Lactantius, *Divine Institutes* 4.1 (PL 6:447–51).

184. H. Clavier, "Problème du rite et du mythe dans le quatrième evangile," *Revue d'histoire et de philosophie religieuses* 31 (1951): 292; Linton, *Das Problem der Urkirchen*, 132–33; Dahl, "Christ, Creation and the Church," 422–43.

185. Ambrose, *Expositio in Lucam (Commentary on Luke)* 2.88 (PL 15:1667–68); Chrysostom, *Homilia in apostolicum dictum: Hoc scitote, quod in novissimis diebus erunt tempora gravia (Homily on the Apostolic Saying: "This know also, that in the last days perilous times shall come" [2 Timothy 3:1])* 5 (PG 56:276).

186. Origen, *Commentary on Matthew* 56 (PG 13:1688D), attacks this view, held by Michael Brunec, "De 'signis prodromis' (Matthew 24:5–13)" and "De magna tribulatione (Matthew 24:15–24)," *Verbum domini* 30 (1952): 265, 269, 277, 323–24.

187. Hippolytus, *On the Consummation of the World* 24–25 (PG 10:937B–C).

188. F. F. Bruce, "Eschatology," *London Quarterly and Holborn Review* 183 (1958): 99, with a survey of the literature, 101–3.

189. Georges Florovsky, "Eschatology in the Patristic Age: An Introduction," in vol. 64 of Texte und Untersuchungen zur Geschichte der altchristlichen Literatur (Berlin: Akademie-Verlag, 1957), 235–38.

190. Oscar Cullmann, "Rudolf Bultmann's Concept of Myth and the New Testament," *Concordia Theological Monthly* 27 (1956): 24; M. Burrows, "Thy Kingdom Come," *Journal of Biblical Literature* 74 (1955): 1–8.

191. Hans J. Schoeps, "Die ebionitische Wahrheit des Christentums," in Davies and Daube, *Background of the New Testament,* 123.

2

Evangelium quadraginta dierum: The Forty-Day Mission of Christ— The Forgotten Heritage

While those who ponder the historical relevance of Acts 1:3 concern themselves almost exclusively with the evidence of the canonical writings, we now possess in the early apocryphal texts, both those recently discovered and those being reappraised in the light of new findings, an impressive body of evidence that has direct bearing on the problem of the historicity of the forty days. It is the purpose of the present study to indicate briefly the nature of this evidence.

The theme of the forty days has always been a disturbing one. For many scholars the possibility of such an event as that indicated in Acts 1:3 is not even to be discussed,[1] for others such things are tolerable only as myths,[2] while some are frank

This article first appeared under the title "Evangelium quadraginta dierum," in *Vigiliae christianae* 20 (1966): 1–24. The article was reprinted under the title "The Forty-Day Mission of Christ—The Forgotten Heritage," in *When the Lights Went Out* (Salt Lake City: Deseret Book, 1970), 33–54, and as "Evangelium quadraginta dierum: The Forty-Day Mission of Christ—The Forgotten Heritage," in *Mormonism and Early Christianity* (Salt Lake City: Deseret Book and FARMS, 1987), 10–44.

enough to admit that they simply don't like the story.[3] It is astonishing how many writers on the resurrection pass by the forty-day interval in studied silence,[4] and indeed churchmen since Clement and Origen have employed all the arts of rhetoric and logic to evade its crass literalism.[5] It is claimed that the story is insufficiently attested,[6] or that the language[7] or the thought-forms of the ancients elude us,[8] or that the writers themselves are confused—for example, in maintaining that "flesh and blood cannot inherit the kingdom" while asserting "the very opposite" in the doctrine of the resurrection.[9] We are often reminded today that we are here dealing with prefigured types and images that need not be taken literally, forty itself being a well-known symbolic number in sacred writings.[10]

But on the other hand, Luke may well have chosen the round number precisely because everybody knew of like forty-day periods of spiritual discipline and preparation;[11] ancient thought-forms can be checked by the words and behavior of an Ignatius, willing to give his life to show how *he* interpreted the forty days;[12] and contradictions may well have their source in the minds of readers rather than writers—the "flesh and blood" issue, in fact, seems to be of our own making.[13]

Yet even those who accept the reality of the forty-day ministry are at a loss to explain it. Plainly, the key is missing when serious commentators can describe the event as a mere "example of condescension and friendship" by one who had more urgent business elsewhere,[14] or as a magnanimous recompense for the forty *hours* of anguish occasioned by the Lord's absence in the tomb,[15] or as a long lingering farewell,[16] or as "forty-odd days of frustration and inaction,"[17] or as a strategic and psychological holding back of forces for a more effective charge on the enemy.[18] It is often claimed that a full forty days were necessary to demonstrate the reality of resurrected flesh,[19] and if that seems odd (forty seconds were sufficient to convince Thomas) we are told that the apostles had to *over*learn their lesson in order to persuade an overskeptical world.[20] The forty days are also described as a weaning process, to draw the disciples away from undue attachment to each other,[21] or to the person of the Lord—lest they be too upset by his departure,[22] or, strangest of all, to wean their minds away from corporeal concepts to the pure realms of disembodied intellect.[23] In short, if anything like the "Great Forty Days" occurred, the enormous portent of it, which Luke puts at the very root of the Christian faith, quite escapes the commentators, who view it as an odd and rather "interesting" interlude[24] but admit that in the end we do *not* know what Christ did or said during the forty days but can only conjecture.[25]

The argument most confidently put forth today for the postresurrectional activity of Jesus is the behavior of the apostles, who before the resurrection were by all accounts unready not only to preach but even to hear "the things of the kingdom" and yet presently went forth into the world fully laden.[26] But is it not remarkable that *nothing* has come down to us from that wonderful time when the church is supposed to have received all its knowledge and training? Why have we only the opening words of the Lord's discourse, declaring how badly the disciples needed the instruction that followed (Luke 24:25–27), of which nothing is preserved in the canon (v. 45)? Those early apocryphal writings which purport to tell the rest of the story may not be ignored by the serious student. These writings take a position of conscious resistance to the rising tide of skepticism regarding the reality of the resurrection.[27] Luke had made it perfectly clear at the outset of his history that he was dealing with solid reality; like his other prologue, the story of Zacharias, this one is a forthright factual account that leaves no margin for speculation. Unlike the related themes of the resurrection and ascension, the forty days has had no appeal to artists and orators, for it offers the imagination nothing to play with—it is not a subject for discussion but an end of discussion, not something to be proven but the proof itself, the unshakable cornerstone of the edifice Luke is about to construct.[28] In this spirit the bulk of the early apocryphal writings make of the forty days the foundation of their own teachings, and when Ignatius wants an unanswerable argument for the resurrection of the flesh, he appeals not only to the forty days but to a non-canonical witness for them.[29]

It is significant that the *favorite* theme of the early apoc-rypha happens to be "the teachings of the Lord to the Apostles after the Resurrection," often directly indicated as such[30] and often indirectly.[31] This has often been interpreted as both a bid for prestige by the various authors and a claim to immunity from criticism.[32] But the tradition could only offer such secu-rity if it enjoyed unquestioned acceptance in the church, and if we examine the actual teachings purveyed under the frank of the forty days it soon becomes apparent that they were never designed to be popular but represent old and very unpopular doctrines in retreat. Even among the first disciples belief in a literal resurrection was only enforced after long resistance,[33] and it proved a *horrendum* to the churchmen ever after.[34] But the most conspicuous teaching of all in the forty-day reper-toire is a picture of the future which cannot be surpassed for unrelieved pessimism and gloom. Here surely is no product of wishful thinking or sly invention.

In a standard forty-day situation the apostles, deeply wor-ried, ask the Lord what lies ahead for them and their work[35] and receive an appalling reply: They are to be rejected by all men and take their violent exit from the world[36] when corrupters and false shepherds will appear within the church, where a growing faction of the worldly minded will soon overcome and annihilate what remains of the faithful saints.[37] The sheep turn into wolves as the Wintertime of the Just settles down;[38] the lights go out and the long age of darkness begins under the rule of the *cosmoplanēs,* disastrously usurping the authority of Christ.[39] There is indeed a promise of comfort and joy, but it is all on the other side and in the distant return of the Lord.[40] The apostles protest, as we do today: Is this a time for speaking of death and disaster?[41] Can all that has transpired be but for the salvation of a few and the condemnation of many? But Jesus remains unyielding: that is not for us to decide or to question.[42] The grim picture is confirmed by the apostolic fathers, who are convinced that they are beholding the fulfillment of these very prophecies and are driven by a tragic sense of urgency and finality.[43] After them the early patristic writers accept the pattern with heavy reluctance,[44] and only the surprising and unexpected victory of the church in the fourth century enables Eusebius's generation to turn the tables and discredit the whole pessimistic tradition.[45]

Nobody would willingly invent such a depressing message or accept it without the highest credentials. The picture, though full of familiar elements from the earlier Jewish apocalypses, is not derived from them. The actors are not prophets and kings of other ages but the very men sitting before the Master; the predictions are not for distant ages but limited to a scope of two generations;[46] and what is described is not the fate of the world or even of Israel, nor titanic upheavals of nature, but the undoing of the Christian society by perverters and corrupters in its midst.[47] The more grandiose imagery is not missing, but it is kept distinct from the story of the church, which is concrete, specific, and utterly gloomy.

All the forty-day teaching is described as very *secret,* delivered to a closed cult group.[48] There is no desire to intrigue and mystify, however, as with the gnostics, but rather the clearly stated policy that knowledge should be given always but only to those who ask for it,[49] with the corollary that the higher and holier a teaching the more carefully it should be guarded.[50] As "the last and highest revelation," the teaching of the forty days was top secret and has not come down to us.[51] Since Irenaeus, churchmen have strenuously denied that there ever was a secret teaching or that anything really important has ever been lost.[52] To profess otherwise would be perilously close to an admission of bankruptcy; yet Christian scholars do concede that the apostles had information that we do not have,[53] allow the existence of an unwritten apostolic tradition in the church,[54] and grant that there was a policy of secrecy in the early church—though insisting that it began with the catechetical schools.[55] The catechists, however, appeal to a much earlier tradition of secrecy,[56] and when the fathers attempt to reproduce the unwritten tradition which they claim for the church they have nothing to offer but the commonplaces of the schools.[57] Plainly, things *have* been lost.

After the alarming gap in the record following the fall of Jerusalem, the curtain rises on a second-century church seething with conflict and split into factions hotly debating the reality of the resurrection.[58] The gnostic exploited both the ignorance and the knowledge of the time—the knowledge that the answers to the great questions of existence were known and treasured by "the elders" of another day, and the ignorance of just what that knowledge was. The oldest definition of the gnosis specifies that it was the knowledge imparted secretly by the Lord to the apostles after the resurrection. The gnostics claimed to have that very knowledge,[59] and their tremendous initial success shows how hungry the Christian world was for it—the "main church," in fact, had to invent a countergnosis of its own to meet the threat and ended up with a compromise that has left a gnostic stamp on Christian thinking ever since.[60] The gnostics did not invent the forty-day situation, as has been claimed, for they were the last people in the world to imagine a return of the Savior in the flesh, and any tinkering would have been readily exposed in a quarreling and hypercritical society; but they did exploit it because it was there and they had to: at a time when everything else was being questioned, it is one of the few things that is never challenged.[61]

The apocryphal teachings of the forty days taken together comprise an imposing doctrinal edifice, totally unlike the patchwork systems of the gnostics. It begins with the most natural question to ask anyone returning to earth after being away: Where did you go and what did you see? The Lord's discourse in reply recalls the journeys to worlds above and below recounted by the prophets and patriarchs of the old Jewish apocrypha.[62] And yet the picture is quite different: They go as observers and report what they have seen, while he goes as a missionary and reports what he has done. The central theme is the descensus, a mission to the spirits below closely resembling the Lord's earthly calling.[63] He brings the *kerygma* to all, and those who accept it follow him out of the depths into the light,[64] receive baptism,[65] and hence mount up by degrees to realms of glory, for as in the Jewish apocrypha the picture of other worlds is not a simple one.[66] This mounting up is depicted as the return of the spirit to its heavenly home, where it existed in glory before coming to earth.[67] This is not the gnostic idea of premortal existence, however, for the soul is not sent down as punishment nor imprisoned in the flesh, nor does it fly directly to God after its release from physical confinement;[68]

rather it is sent to be tried and tested in "the blessed vessel" of the flesh whose immortality is guaranteed by the resurrection.[69]

There is a strong emphasis in early Christian literature on the doctrine of the Two Ways, depicting life as a time of probation, a constant confrontation with good and evil and the obligation to choose between them.[70] This is conceived as part of a plan laid down "in the presence of the first angels" at the creation of the world,[71] according to which through Adam's fall the human race would be placed in the position, envied by the angels, of being perfectly free to choose good or evil and thereby fully merit whatever rewards would follow.[72] Satan rebelled against the plan, refused obeisance to Adam, and was cast down upon the earth with his cohorts to fulfill divine purpose by providing, as "the serpent," the temptation necessary for an effectual testing of human beings.[73] Through inspired prophets, men from time to time are taught the rules of the game but are prone to cheat, fall away into darkness, and require painful correction before returning to divine favor and a new dispensation of heavenly gifts and covenants.[74] The historical picture is a complicated one, culminating in the final return of the Lord, but not before he has made other appearances, notably to a few "righteous and pure souls and faithful," preparatory to the ultimate and glorious parousia.[75]

What gives substance to this peculiar doctrinal structure is the imposing body of rites and ordinances that goes with it.[76] Ritual and doctrinal elements are inextricably interwoven in a complex in which everything is oddly literal and all fit solidly together: The *kerygma*, whether above or below, is real and must have a "seal," which is baptism, though the word is also used to designate rites of washing and anointing that go with it;[77] after such rites the initiate receives a symbolic but real and tangible garment,[78] and then sits down to a sacral meal, a real repast celebrating the perfect unity of the participants with each other and with the Lord, who is present in spirit.[79] Recent findings indicate unusual emphasis placed on a perfect unity of the sexes in marriage ordinances which were real enough and secret enough to excite the scandalized speculations of outsiders[80] and the fantastic imitation of the gnostics.[81] After all allowances have been made, there remains a definite residue of early Christian ritual that goes far beyond anything known to later Christianity, which admittedly got its liturgy from the synagogue and the Hellenistic world, while the rites just mentioned all look to the temple and belong to the instructions of the forty days.[82]

While the schools have their methods for dealing with unwelcome doctrines and traditions, the populace also has ways of absorbing and adapting teachings it does not understand, and the forty-day tradition left a bold imprint on vulgar Christianity. The fact that the Christian liturgy has always allowed a forty-day interval, and an important one, between the resurrection and the ascension is not to be lightly explained away,[83] but it is the popular literature of the pseudo-Acts of the Apostles and the legends of the martyrs that most clearly indicate what was paramount in the teachings embraced by the newly converted masses of the age of Constantine.[84] Here we have the monotonous repetition as one standard miracle, the raising of the dead, is performed to demonstrate to a skeptical world the reality of the resurrection of Jesus.[85] As the saint performs this miracle, or has it performed on him, Jesus himself stands by, now in his own person, now in that of the apostle, who is but his double or understudy.[86] This, it is often explained, is what Jesus meant when he said he would continue to be with the apostles to the end—it is a series of real appearances continuing the personal tutelage and supervision of the forty days.[87]

The secular equivalent to this is the recurring legend of a youthful military hero and convert who is repeatedly put to death with spectacular tortures, only to be visited by Christ or the angels in the night and restored to health, ready to deliver a lecture on the resurrection and renew his painful demonstrations on the following day. His resuscitation is celebrated sometimes with the Eucharist and often with a great public banquet.[88] The saints Victor, Theodore, George, Mercurius, Sebastian[89] and the Seven Sleepers,[90] as well as the first lady martyrs, Thecla, Felicitas, and Perpetua,[91] belong to this illustrious company to which the names of most of the apostles were added.[92]

Recurrent motifs in the legends, such as their strongly erotic orientation and the prominence of feasting, games, holy springs, horses and chariots, etc., point unmistakably to popular pre-Christian hero-cults,[93] typical of which is the cult of the chaste Hippolytus, impaled on a tree and restored to life, whose "tragic death and triumphant resurrection made him a favorite theme alike on Greek and Roman sarcophagi."[94] It is well known that local heroes and their cults were often converted to Christianity, but why the emphasis on a particular type of hero to the neglect of others, and how could the Christians bring themselves to make such concessions to the familiar ways of heathen idolatry? It was not because the Christian tradition was derived from the other—we know now that the two were quite different—but because there were definite points of resemblance at which they could fuse. Thus Puech and Quispel have recently pointed to the pagan origin of the cloud and chariot of apotheosis, a conspicuous object in our forty-day accounts.[95] But their well-known pagan affinities would have rendered them invincibly repugnant to the Christians had they not something of their own that closely matched the pagan version. And what that was is apparent on every other page of the legends, where Jesus himself breaks into the story to give his instructions and then mount up to heaven "in great glory." Again, how could the panegyrics and protocol of the imperial cult, hailing the Christian emperor as *praesens et corporalis deus,* appear as anything but blasphemous unless there was a Christian precedent for them?[96] We see that precedent in the constant intervention of Christ and his angels in the solemn assemblies of the emperor and on the field of battle; the clouds and angels that surround the august personage are the familiar properties not of the schools but of the monks of the desert, who sought to recapture the ancient order of the church and who still thought of Christ as paying frequent and familiar visits to holy men.[97] In the safely theatrical displays of rhetoric and architecture, the forty-day idea of God mingling with men and supervising their affairs in person was carried over as a basic Christian concept into the new popular Christianity.

The easiest way of disposing of the forty-day problem is to point out the numerous parallels and prefigurements to it, taking as evidence of fraud what the early Christians regarded as the sure stamp of authenticity. Easter, ascension, Pentecost, transfiguration, and even parousia are depicted today as "one undifferentiated experience," or at least as "different ways of describing the same occurrence," which naturally leaves no room for the awkward interruption of the forty days.[98]

But a process need not be instantaneous, indeed cannot be, and gaps and delays are required if only to allow some time for preaching to the human family, while the idea that the Messiah can appear only once denies the fundamental thesis of Christianity and was, in fact, the principal obstacle to the acceptance of Jesus by the Jews.[99] Moreover, if uniqueness is the mark of a historical event, the forty days commands the highest respect. It is recognized today that the very oddness of Jesus' teachings is strong proof of authenticity. No group of men, it is argued, would come together and of their own volition fashion doctrines that were "a slap in the face . . . to everything that healthy human understanding has viewed as sound thinking from that day to this."[100] What is more, no one would *accept* the incredible reports about the risen Lord unless "facts forced them to it."[101] The argument applies with particular force to the absolutely unparalleled situation of the forty days, when Christ, "immortal and glorious," condescends "to come to the table of illiterate and poor Apostles, partake of their coarse fare while he sits chatting with them" in a middle-class tenement or beside a smoky fire on the beach.[102]

The one thing that has got a respectful hearing for the forty-day ministry is the need for such an episode to explain the founding of the church. Catholic theologians especially favor it as a time for settling all doctrinal issues, establishing proper officials, and preparing the apostles for a missionary activity which the world was to find irresistible.[103] But we have already noted that the progress of the church was but a triumphal process "*out* of the world"[104] and that nothing was ever handed down from that great time of instruction, conventional Christianity having rejected all the traditions of the forty days and turned elsewhere for its doctrine and liturgy.[105] The church can hardly claim the forty days as its franchise while confessing total ignorance of what was done and taught at that time.[106]

To summarize, then, we have in the early apocryphal writings both direct and indirect evidence for the reality of the postresurrectional activity of Jesus. (1) By uniformly supporting the clear and unequivocal language of Acts 1:3, and by making the forty-day teaching their principal concern, these writers serve notice that this subsequently despised and neglected theme had top priority among the early Christians. (2) Under the heading of the forty-day conversations, the same writings convey to us a consistent and closely knit body of doctrine (3) accompanied by an equally organic structure of rites and ordinances—*not* a farrago of odds and ends in the gnostic manner.[107] (4) The gnostic phenomenon itself attests the universal awareness that such a teaching had formerly existed and been lost to the main church: the specific gnostic claim to possess the secrets of the forty days shows what it was that was missing. (5) Furthermore, the apocryphal writings themselves fully explain that loss in terms of both secrecy and apostasy, while (6) the great impact of the forty-day image on popular Christianity is clearly reflected in popular legends and cults.

As indirect evidence we must consider the extreme oddness and unpopularity of the forty-day proposition, logically and artistically disturbing and burdened with a view of the future which is negative and frightening. It is anything but a product of wishful thinking or a bid for popular support. Yet the only arguments against it have been arguments of interpretation. Over against a facile manipulation of tests stands a massive array of phenomena which deserves more than the wave of the hand which we have given it here. Why is there no *Evangelium quadraginta dierum?* Its absence confirms the unreality of the forty days to those scholars who point out that the record speaks only of what Christ *taught* during that period rather than what he *did*.[108] But as Anselm observes, before the resurrection Christ was human—after it he was God.[109] As such he came to teach and to teach only—all are agreed that even the eating and drinking had no other purpose—communing with men on a wholly different level from the man of sorrows in the Gospels. The forty-day episode is indeed unique. If it never took place, what was it that produced the singular phenomena that have been attributed to it?

Notes

1. "We are bound to conclude that such an occurrence is not only improbable but impossible." John G. Davies, *He Ascended into Heaven* (New York: Association Press, 1958), quotation on 56; generally 54–60. Cf. Erich Grässer, "Die Apostelgeschichte in der Forschung der Gegenwart," *Theologische Rundschau* 26 (1960): 101. "So hat die Gemeinde . . . gedichtet und gewoben." Wilhelm Bousset, *Kyrios Christos* (Göttingen: Vandenhoeck and Ruprecht, 1926), 74.

2. To be taken "seriously, but not literally." M. J. Suggs, quoting Richard R. Niebuhr, in "Biblical Eschatology and the Message of the Church," *Encounter* 24 (1963): 18–19. "Das können wir zwar nicht zusammendenken, aber die Evangelisten konnten es." David F. Strauss, *Das Leben Jesu,* 9th ed. (Leipzig: Brockhaus, 1864), 2:151–52. "We can only know Jesus clad in the garb of myth." Joachim Jeremias, "The Present Position in the Controversy Concerning the Problem of the Historical Jesus," *Expository Times* 69 (1958): 334–35.

3. "Half of it I like, and half of it I don't." P. Scherer, "Then Came Jesus and Stood in the Midst: A Sermon," *Interpretation* 12 (1958): 56. "The point is, do we or do we not like the answers?" Murdoch E. Dahl, *The Resurrection of the Body* (London: SCM Press, 1962), 92.

4. For example, Severus of Antioch fails to mention the forty days in his exhaustive treatise on the resurrection, in M.-A. Kugener and Edgar Triffaux, eds. and trans., "Les homilia cathédrales de Sevère d'Antioche: Homélie LXXVII" (PO 16:794–862), as does Bousset, *Kyrios Christos,* 74; and Dahl, *Resurrection of the Body,* 92; also Frederick J. Foakes-Jackson and Kirsopp Lake, *Commentary on Acts* (London: Macmillan, 1939); and Grässer in his long survey, "Apostelgeschichte," 92–167. Even John F. Walvoord's carefully prepared list of seventeen postresurrection appearances of Jesus, "The Earthly Life of the Incarnate Christ," *Bibliotheca sacra* 117 (1960): 298–300, fails to mention the forty days.

5. Discussed by Carl Schmidt, *Gespräche Jesu mit seinen Jüngern nach der Auferstehung* (Leipzig: Hinrichs, 1919), 524–29.

6. Thus Davies, *He Ascended into Heaven*, 56–60; S. MacLean Gilmour, "Easter and Pentecost," *Journal of Biblical Literature* 81 (1962): 63–64.

7. Ed. Schweitzer, "Die hellenistichen Komponente im neutestamentlichen Sarx-Begriff," *Zeitschrift für die neutestamentliche Wissenschaft* 48 (1957): 250–53; B. Holt, "Realities of the Ascension," *Encounter* 24 (1963): 88, 90.

8. "It is unlikely that the Apostle's [Paul's] logic bore any resemblance to ours, whether deductive or inductive." Dahl, *Resurrection of the Body*, 23. See Rudolf Bultmann, *Das Verhältnis der urchristlichen Christusbotschaft zum historischen Jesus* (Heidelberg: Winter, 1960): 24; Davies, *He Ascended into Heaven*, 57; and G. Lindeskog, "Christuskerygma und Jesustradition," *Novum Testamentum* 5 (1961–62): 144.

9. Kirsopp and Silva Lake, *An Introduction to the New Testament* (New York: Harper, 1937), 46–47. John and Paul were both confused about postresurrectional realities; see Gilmour, "Easter and Pentecost," 62–63.

10. Davies, *He Ascended into Heaven*, 52–53. On forty days as a symbol, see Frederick J. Foakes-Jackson, *The Acts of the Apostles* (New York: Harper, 1931), 5:2; and Pierre Miquel, "Christ's Ascension and Our Glorification," *Theology Digest* 9 (1961): 68. See also note 98 below.

11. P. A. van Stempvoort, "The Interpretation of the Ascension in Luke and Acts," *New Testament Studies* 5 (1958): 33–34, 39–41, shows that for Luke the designation of forty days signifies simply "that the appearances of Christ after Easter had a certain duration." Most commentators note that the *parestēsen heauton* of Acts 1:3 indicates occasional appearances over a period of time. Hence it would be impossible and foolish to calculate the exact length of the postresurrectional sojourn. Even Hilary, *Commentarius in Matthaeum (Commentary on*

Matthew) 3 (PL 9:928), is quite aware of the symbolic propriety of the forty-day expression.

12. Ignatius, *Epistola ad Trallianos (Epistle to the Trallians)* 10 (PG 5:681), and *Epistola ad Smyrnaeos (Epistle to the Smyrnaeans)* 2–3 (PG 5:708–9).

13. The contradictions are discussed by C. F. D. Moule, "The Ascension—Acts 1:9," *Expository Times* 68 (1957): 205–9. "The blood is the life," but specifically the earthly life. H. W. Robinson, "Blood," in *Encyclopaedia of Religion and Ethics,* ed. James Hastings (New York: Scribner, 1908–26), 2:715–16. The mention of blood is pointedly omitted in Luke 24:39, being nowhere ascribed to resurrected beings. Cf. Hippolytus, *Sermonum sive homiliarum fragmenta (Fragments of Sermons or Homilies)* 1 (PG 10:861).

14. Cornelius à Lapide [C. van den Steen], *Commentaria in scripturam sacram* (Paris: Coen, 1877), 18:51.

15. Hildebert, *Sermons on Time* 48.471 (PL 171:579); Lapide, *Commentaria,* 18:48–49, gives other sources.

16. Lapide, *Commentaria,* 18:50.

17. F. R. Hancock, "The Man of Galilee," *Hibbert Journal* 57 (1958–59): 223.

18. Chrysostom, *Commentarius in Acta Apostolorum (Commentary on the Acts of the Apostles)* 1.4 (PG 60:18–20); Theophylactus, *Expositio in Acta Apostolorum (Exposition of the Acts of the Apostles)* 1.8 (PG 125:508).

19. Leo Magnus, *Sermo (Discourse)* 73 [71] (PL 54:394–96); Ernaldus, *De carnalibus operibus Christi (On the Mortal Works of Christ)* 11 (PL 189:1667–68); Lapide, *Commentaria,* 18:51.

20. Chrysostom, *Commentary on the Acts of the Apostles* 1.5 (PG 60:19–20); and F. F. Bruce, *The Acts of the Apostles* (London: Tyndale, 1962), 67–68.

21. Miquel, "Christ's Ascension," 71.

22. William Jenks, ed., *Supplement to the Comprehensive Commentary on the Holy Bible* (Brattleboro, Vt.: Fessenden, 1838), 5:4.

23. Ernaldus, *On the Mortal Works of Christ* 11 (PL 189: 1667–68); Lapide, *Commentaria,* 18:49.

24. "The conversations of the Great Forty Days must have been of intensest interest, yet . . . these things are wrapped about with thickest darkness." M. Dods, R. Watson, F. Farrar, eds., *An Exposition of the Bible* (Hartford: Scranton, 1903–4), 5:302. "A great deal more passed on those most interesting subjects . . . than is anywhere recorded." Matthew Henry and Thomas Scott, *Commentary on the Holy Bible* (London: Religious Tract Society, 1866), vol. 5, at Acts 1:3.

25. "Just what does a spiritual body do? We do not know." Eugène Jacquier, *Les actes des apôtres,* 2nd ed. (Paris: Librairie Victor Lecoffre, 1926), 7–8. "We can only reverently conjecture." Charles J. Ellicott, *Commentary on the Whole Bible* (Grand Rapids: Zondervan, 1954), 7, at Acts 1:3. "Nowhere set forth in the Scriptures . . . impertinent to inquire and over-bold to specify." Lapide, *Commentaria,* 18:49.

26. Discussed by J. Schneider, "Der Beitrag der Urgemeinde zur Jesusüberlieferung im Lichte der neuesten Forschung," *Theologische Literaturzeitung* 87 (1962): 401–12.

27. Michel Testuz, ed., *Papyrus Bodmer X: Correspondance apocryphe des Corinthiens et de l'apôtre Paul* 51:11, 54:24, 55:24–30, 56:31–35 (Cologne: Bibliotheca Bodmeriana, 1959), 33, 39, 41, 43; the same in the Acts of Paul 7; see Leon Vouaux, trans. and comm., *Les actes de Paul et ses lettres apocryphes* (Paris: Letouzey et Ané, 1913), 158–59; cf. Polycarp, *Epistola ad Philippenses (Epistle to the Philippians)* 7.1 (PG 5:1012); *Gospel of the Twelve Apostles* 13–14 (PO 2:168–69); *Gospel of Philip* 105:9–14 (=NHL 57:9–14, p. 134); Clement, *Epistola I ad Corinthios (First Epistle to the Corinthians)* 24–27 (PG 1:260–69); Clement, *Epistola II ad Corinthios (Second Epistle to the Corinthians)* 9–12 (PG 1:341–47); Ignatius, *Epistola ad Magnesios (Epistle to the Magnesians)* 11 (PG 5:670); Ignatius, *Epistle to the Trallians* 9–10 (PG 5:669–72); Ignatius, *Epistle to the Smyrnaeans* 2–3 (PG 5:708–9); Barnabas, *Epistola catholica (Catholic Epistle)* 5–6 (PG 2:733–44); Shepherd of Hermas, *Similitudo (Similitudes)* 5.7

(PG 2:961–62); *Constitutiones apostolicae (Apostolic Constitutions)* 6.26 (PG 1:976–77); *Revelation to Peter,* in E. Verdapet, "The Revelation of the Lord to Peter," *Zeitschrift für die neutestamentliche Wissenschaft* 23 (1924): 14; *Epistle of the Apostles* 19 (30), 21 (32), 25 (36) (Copt. xii, xiv, xix) (*ANT,* 491–94); *Apocalypse of Peter* (*ANT,* 512–13); *Apocalypse of Thomas* (*ANT,* 561); *Apocryphon of James* 11:35–12:17 (=*NHL,* p. 34); cf. Athenogoras, *De resurrectione mortuorum (On the Resurrection of the Dead)* (PG 6:973–1024); *Odes of Solomon* 22:9–10 (*OTP* 2:755).

28. "St. Luke . . . gives to his narrative something of the seal of a medical statement." James J. J. Tissot, *Life of Our Lord Jesus Christ* (New York: McClure-Tissot, 1899), 4:257. "No metaphysical or psychological explanation can be given." Hugh V. White, "Immortality and Resurrection in Recent Theology," *Encounter* 22 (1961): 56–57.

29. Ignatius, *Epistle to the Smyrnaeans* 3.2 (PG 5:709), from an old Gospel of the Hebrews, according to Jerome, *De viris illustribus (On Noted Men),* prologue and chapter 16 (PL 23:633, 655), though Eusebius, *Historia ecclesiastica (Ecclesiastical History)* 3.36.11 (PG 20:289), does not know the source.

30. *Testament in Galilee* 1.45 (the Ethiopian version of the *Epistola apostolorum*) (PO 9:177, 216); also in Schmidt, *Gespräche Jesu,* 26–27; this work can also be found in *ANT,* 485–503, and in Edgar Hennecke, *New Testament Apocrypha,* ed. Wilhelm Schneemelcher and Robert McL. Wilson (Philadelphia: Westminister, 1963–65), 1:189–226; *Apocryphon of James* 2:19–26, 8:1–4, discussed by H. Puech and G. Quispel, "Les écrits gnostiques du Codex Jung," *Vigiliae christianae* 8 (1954): 8; *Acts of Thomas* 1; "Les écrits gnostiques du Codex Jung," in *Testamentum Domini nostri Jesu Christi (Testament of Our Lord Jesus Christ),* ed. Ignatius E. Rahmani (Mainz: Kirchheim, 1899), 1, prologue; *Gospel of the Twelve Apostles* 14 (PO 2:169–70); *Gospel of Bartholomew* (PO 2:190–91, 194); and fragments in André Wilmart and Eugene Tisserant, "Fragments grecs et latins de l'évangile de

Barthélemy," *Revue biblique* 22 n.s. 10 (1913): 185; Oxyrhynchus Logia, no. 8 (1); Freer Logion (*ANT,* 34); *Book of the Resurrection of Christ by Barnabas the Apostle* (*ANT,* 185).

31. It has been shown that the term the *Living Jesus* (and even *kyrios*) refers specifically to the risen Lord. Schmidt, *Gespräche Jesu,* 264; cf. James R. Harris, *The Odes and Psalms of Solomon: Now First Published from the Syriac Version* (Cambridge: Cambridge University Press, 1909), 73. Thus the same value must be given to the opening line of the *Gospel of Thomas* 80:10 (=*NHL* 32:10, p. 118), as to the Oxyrhynchus Logia, no. 8 (1): "sayings which Jesus who liveth and was dead spake to Judas Thomas"; cf. *Gospel of Thomas* 99:7–8 (=*NHL* 51:7–8, p. 129). The conversational and questioning form of discourse is another clue. Schmidt, *Gespräche Jesu,* 206; Puech and Quispel, "Les écrits gnostiques du Codex Jung," 9 n. 3; *Gospel of Thomas* 81:14–17 (=*NHL* 33:14–17, p. 118); Oxyrhynchus Logia, 4–5, 13 (6), 8 (1); a large number of the pseudo Acts in E. A. Wallis Budge, *Contendings of the Apostles* (Oxford: Oxford University Press, 1935), begin with the apostles questioning Christ after the resurrection. Where an account of the resurrection or descensus is included in the report the setting is naturally postresurrectional: this refers to all the apocrypha mentioned below, notes 63–66. The forty-day situation is implied where the resurrection of others is described, as in the second Akhmim fragment of the *Gospel of Peter* (*ANT,* 508); *Gospel of the Twelve Apostles* 2 (PO 2:135); and *Acts of Thomas* 54–55 (*ANT,* 390–91). The prologue to the *Discourse on Abbatôn* purports to offer documentary evidence from the hands of the apostles for the typical forty-day situation it describes, in E. A. Wallis Budge, *Coptic Martyrdoms* (1914; reprint, New York: AMS, 1977), 225–26, 474–75.

32. Schmidt, *Gespräche Jesu,* 201–6.

33. Matthew 28:17; Mark 16:8, 11–14; Luke 24:11, 21–35, 21–43; John 20:9, 25–29.

34. Schmidt, *Gespräche Jesu,* 346–47.

35. "Let us know what is the end of the aeon for we stand in the midst of scandals and offenses." *Gospel of the Twelve Apostles* (PO 2:160); *Apocryphon of James,* see Puech and Quispel, "Les écrits gnostiques du Codex Jung," 12–15; *Gospel of Thomas* 82:25 (=NHL 34:25, p. 119); *Testament in Galilee* 1:4, 40, 43, 45, 47–48, 51, 61; *Revelation to Peter,* in Vardapet, "The Revelation of the Lord to Peter," 12; *Epistle of the Apostles* 17 (28); 19 (30); cf. *Testament of Moses* 11 (*OTP* 1:933–34); *Testament of Our Lord Jesus Christ* 2; *Apocalypse of Peter* (*ANT,* 510–11).

36. For a general treatment, see Hugh W. Nibley, "The Passing of the Primitive Church," in *Mormonism and Early Christianity* (Salt Lake City: Deseret Book and FARMS, 1987), 169–74 (pages 2–7 in this volume).

37. The two parties are the righteous *thlibomenoi* and the wicked *thlibontes.* Herbert Braun, "Zur nachpaulinischen Herkunft des zweiten Thessalonischerbriefes," *Zeitschrift für die neutestamentliche Wissenschaft* 44 (1952–53): 152–54. "They will combine against those who love me, to hate them and push them aside as nothing." *Epistle of the Apostles* 50 (61) (*ANT,* 503); *Testament of Our Lord Jesus Christ* 1:13. "The idea that the just are going to be persecuted by the wicked" is found in the *Testament in Galilee,* and Clement, *First Epistle to the Corinthians* 1, 3–6, 45–47, and 57 (PG 1:205–8, 213–21, 299–308, 324–25); see L. Guerrier, "Avant-Propos," in *Testament in Galilee* (PO 9:145).

38. On the wolves, see Ignatius, *Epistola ad Philadelphenses (Epistle to the Philadelphians)* 2 (PG 5:820); Clement, *Second Epistle to the Corinthians* 5 (PG 1:336); *Didache* 16, in Kirsopp Lake, *Apostolic Fathers,* LCL (Cambridge: Harvard University Press, 1912), 1:332; *1 Enoch* 89:13–27, 51–75; 90 (*OTP* 1:65–72); cf. *Epistle of the Apostles* 50 (61), discussed by Schmidt, *Gespräche Jesu,* 197–98. On the Wintertime, see Shepherd of Hermas, *Similitudes* 3–4 (PG 2:955–58); and Charles Wessely, ed. and trans., "Les plus anciens

monuments du christianisme écrits sur papyrus" (PO 18:469–70); Barnabas, *Catholic Epistle* 15.5 (PG 2:772); *Apocalypse of Baruch (=2 Baruch)* 21:22–24 (*OTP* 1:628); *Gospel of Philip* 100:25–35 (=*NHL* 52:25–35, p. 132), cf. 112:5–10 (=*NHL* 64:5–10, p. 138). The same imagery of the seasons in Eusebius, *De laudibus Constantini (In Praise of Constantine)* 17 (PG 20:1432–33); Cyril of Alexandria, *Commentarius in Joannis Evangelium (Commentary on John)* 4.14 (PG 73:617–18, 620); E. W. Brooks, "A Collection of Letters of Severus of Antioch," no. 81 (PO 14:130); *Gospel of Thomas* 84:22–23 (=*NHL* 36:22–23, p. 120); 1QS *(Manual of Discipline)* IV, 18–19; TB *Pesaḥim* 2a.

39. This is the most conspicuous theme in all the Apocrypha: *Testament in Galilee* 1:3–6; Michaël Asin de Palacios, ed. and trans., "Logia et Agrapha Domini Jesus," no. 115 (PO 19:542–43); Sylvain Grébaut, *Les miracles de Jésus* (PO 17:827–29); *Odes of Solomon* 38:9–15 (*OTP* 2:767); *Ascension of Isaiah* 3:19–4:5 (=*Testament of Hezekiah*, a Christian work) (*OTP* 2:160–61); Clement, *First Epistle to the Corinthians* 2–5 (PG 1:209–20); Ignatius, *Epistola ad Ephesios (Epistle to the Ephesians)* 17 (PG 5:657); Ignatius, *Epistle to the Philadelphians* 2–3 (PG 5:697–700); Barnabas, *Catholic Epistle* 16.19–27 (PG 2:773); *Apostolic Constitutions* 7.32 (PG 1:1021–24); *Didache* 16, in Lake, *Apostolic Fathers*, 1:332; *1 Enoch* 89:10–27 (*OTP* 1:65–66); *Sibylline Oracles* 3 and 4.49 (*OTP* 1:385); *Secrets of Enoch* ([Slavonic] *2 Enoch*) 34 (*OTP* 1:158–59); *2 Baruch* 27–30; 48:32–43; 70 (*OTP* 1:630–631, 637, 644–45); *4 Ezra* 5:1–13; 9:1–13; 10:1–54 (*OTP* 1:531–32, 544–48); *Testament of Our Lord Jesus Christ* 8; *Testament of Moses* 5:1–6 (*OTP* 1:929–30); *Epistle of the Apostles* 36–45 (*ANT*, 498–502); *Apocryphon of Thomas* 1 (*ANT*, 556–58); Akhmim and Freer fragments (*ANT*, 507–8); *Book of John the Evangelist* (*ANT*, 191–93).

40. "To these afflictions on earth corresponds the song of triumph in Heaven." E. Fascher, "Gottes Königtum im Urchristentum," *Numen* 4 (1957): 113. "Through their faithfulness unto death they will attain

to the glory of God, which is their true destiny." Willem C. van Unnik, *Newly Discovered Gnostic Writings* (Naperville, Ill.: Allenson, 1960), 84. "Joyeuses promesses mêlées de menaces affligeantes, trop de sentiments contradictoires." Puech and Quispel, "Les écrits gnostiques du Codex Jung," 15.

41. See Puech and Quispel, "Les écrits gnostiques du Codex Jung," 6, 10, 12, on *Apocryphon of James* 5:28–16:11; *Epistle of the Apostles* 36 (47, Copt. viii–ix) (*ANT,* 498); Clement, *Second Epistle to the Corinthians* 5 (Peter protests) (PG 1:336; cf. *1 Enoch* 89:68–71); Verdapet, "The Revelation of the Lord to Peter," 12.

42. *Testament in Galilee* 4.51, 54, 56 (PO 9:223, 225, 227); *2 Baruch* 55:2–8 (*OTP* 1:640); just so Moses in *Apocalypse of Paul,* in E. A. Wallis Budge, *Miscellaneous Coptic Texts* (1915; reprint, New York: AMS, 1977), 553–54, 1074; *1 Enoch* 89:69, 75–77 (*OTP* 1:68–69). There is a special treatment in *4 Ezra* 5:28–40; 6:59; 7:46; 8:1–3, 14–15 (*OTP* 1:533, 536, 538, 542). The answer is always the same: *Testament in Galilee* 4.42–43, 56 (PO 9:212–14, 227–28); *1 Enoch* 89:75; *2 Baruch* 69:2–4, 75; *4 Ezra* 5:40; 7:60–61; 8:47, 55–56 (*OTP* 1:533, 538–39, 543–44); *Epistle of the Apostles* 19 (30) (*ANT,* 491–92).

43. To the testimony of the apostolic fathers, Nibley, "Passing of the Primitive Church," 173–74 (pages 6–7 in this volume), add Asin de Palacios, "Logia et Agrapha," nos. 108, 115 (PO 19:539, 542); *Psalms of Solomon* 8 (*Odes of Solomon* 51/50), 15–17 (*OTP* 2:658–60, 664–69); Testuz, *Papyrus Bodmer X,* 52, p. 35; *Apocalypse of Paul,* in Budge, *Miscellaneous Coptic Texts,* 540–42, 1060–61; and *Acts of Thecla (Acts of Paul),* cited in Schmidt, *Gespräche Jesu,* 196. *Testament of Hezekiah* (=*Ascension of Isaiah*) describes "the worldliness and lawlessness which prevailed" in the church. R. H. Charles, *Apocrypha and Pseudepigrapha of the Old Testament* (Oxford: Clarendon, 1913), 2:155; Ephraim, *Asketikon,* in Budge, *Coptic Martyrdoms,* 163–64, 415–16, is very close to Clement, *First Epistle to the Corinthians,* and the Shepherd of Hermas; *127 Canons of the Apostles* 12 (PO 8:582–83);

Testament in Galilee 1.3, 6–9 (PO 9:177–78, 183–86); *Testament of Our Lord Jesus Christ* 8.

44.   So Justin, *Dialogus cum Tryphone (Dialogue with Trypho)* 110 (PG 6:493); Origen, *Commentaria in Evangelium secundum Matthaeum (Commentary on Matthew)* 36–38 (PG 13:1650–53); Hippolytus, *Fragmenta in Danielem (Fragments on Daniel)* 38–40 (PG 10:664–65); and Hippolytus, *Scholia in Danielem* 12.1 (PG 10:688); Lactantius, *Divinae institutiones (Divine Institutes)* 4.30 (PL 6:540–44); 5.6 (PL 6:567–69); 7.17 (PL 6:793–95); Irenaeus, *Contra haereses (Against Heresies)* 5.30.1 (PG 7:1203); cf. Irenaeus, *Against Heresies* 4.34.4 (PG 7:1086); Ephraim, *Asketikon,* in Budge, *Coptic Martyrdoms,* 163–64, 415–16. "It is as if the Main Church had a premonition of its demise which constantly and ceaselessly resounds through the early writings." R. Abramowski, "Der Christus der Salomooden," *Zeitschrift für die neutestamentliche Wissenschaft* 35 (1936): 69 n. 41.

45.   Nibley, "Passing of the Primitive Church," 174–76 (pages 8–10 in this volume).

46.   These things happen not to the apostles but to the second generation after them. *Testament in Galilee* 1.4 (PO 9:178–81); so Shepherd of Hermas, *Similitudes* 9.14, 10.4 (PG 2:994, 1012); cf. Asin de Palacios, "Logia et Agrapha," no. 224 (PO 19:601); Hegesippus in Eusebius, *Ecclesiastical History* 3.32 (PG 20:281); *Epistle of the Apostles* 34 (45) (*ANT,* 497). Paul is "the last of the last who will preach to the heathen." Schmidt, *Gespräche Jesu,* 187; cf. 1 Corinthians 4:9–13, and Origen, *Contra Celsum (Against Celsus)* 4.22 (PG 11:1056–57); Wilhelm Nestle, "Zur altchristlichen Apologetik im Neuen Testament," *Zeitschrift für Religions- und Geistesgeschichte* 4 (1952): 118–19.

47.   Schmidt, *Gespräche Jesu,* 385, notes that there is no mention whatever of the pagans as a source of danger or discomfort; it is the believers themselves who turn into betrayers and "enemies of righteousness." *Epistle of the Apostles* 35, 37, 44 (*ANT,* 497–98,

510). A clear distinction is made between the immediate end and the end of the world. *Epistle of the Apostles* 34 (*ANT,* 497); *1 Enoch* 1:2; Schmidt, *Gespräche Jesu,* 102, 339, 484, comments on this.

48. For example, "These are the secret sayings which the living Jesus spoke." *Gospel of Thomas* 80:10 (=*NHL* 32:10, p. 118). Since apocrypha are by definition secret writings, citations are not necessary. Even the "canonical traditions record appearances only to believers" during the forty days. E. C. Rust, "Interpreting the Resurrection," *Journal of Bible and Religion* 29 (1961): 27–28.

49. Matthew 7:8 following 7:6; so *Gospel of Truth* 19:4–18 (=*NHL,* p. 39); *Recognitiones Clementinae* (*Clementine Recognitions*) 3.53, 58 (PG 1:1305, 1307); *Gospel of Thomas* 96:30–34 (=*NHL* 48:30–34, p. 128); 80:12–19 (=*NHL* 32:12–19, p. 118); 81:10–14 (=*NHL* 33:10–14, p. 118); 88:16–18 (=*NHL* 40:16–18, p. 122); 91:34–92:1 (=*NHL* 43:34–44:1, pp. 124–25); Tatian, *Orationes* (*Orations*) 6 (PG 6:817). See next note.

50. It can only damage even Christians who are not prepared for it: 1 Corinthians 3:2; Hebrews 5:12–13; Ignatius, *Epistle to the Trallians* 5 (PG 5:781); *Clementine Recognitions* 2.60 (PG 1:1276–77); Clement of Alexandria, *Stromata* 1.1 (PG 8:704). The highest is achieved by the fewest: *Gospel of Thomas* 94:9–13 (=*NHL* 46:9–13; p. 126); *Gospel of Truth* 21:3–6 (=*NHL,* p. 40); *Gospel of Philip* 105:32–106:10 (=*NHL* 57:32–58:10, p. 135); *Clementine Recognitions* 1.23 (PG 1:1219); 1.28 (PG 1:1222); 1.52 (PG 1:1236); 3.3 (PG 1:1283); 3.34 (PG 1:1297); 4.25 (PG 1:1324–25); *4 Ezra* 14:44–46 (*OTP* 1:555); *Testament of Our Lord Jesus Christ* 1:18; Clement of Alexandria, *Stromata* 5.10 (PG 9:93–101); *Gospel of Bartholomew* 66–68 (*ANT,* 179–80); *Apocalypse of Peter* (*ANT,* 520); *Apocryphon of James* 1:8–25 (=*NHL,* p. 30).

51. At this time the apostles with some embarrassment ask questions which they have never asked before. *Testament in Galilee* 3.31, 4.35 (PO 9:204–5, 207); *Epistle of the Apostles* 20 (31), 24 (35),

25 (36) (*ANT,* 492–95); *Gospel of Bartholomew* 4–5 (*ANT,* 173–81); *Gospel of the Twelve Apostles* (PO 2:135); cf. Jerome, *Dialogus contra Pelagianos (Dialogue against the Pelagians)* 2.15 (PL 23:576–77). They are chided for asking too much, *Apocryphon of James* 2:33–39 (=NHL, p. 30); *Epistle of the Apostles* 25 (36); but are told "the last and highest teachings," *Discourse on Abbatôn,* in Budge, *Coptic Martyrdoms,* 231–32, 480; *Gospel of the Twelve Apostles* (PO 2:160–61); *Epistle of the Apostles* 12 (23): "great and amazing and real things." *Acts of Thomas* 36 (*ANT,* 382); *Gospel of Bartholomew,* fragment in Wilmart and Tisserant, "Fragmenta grecs et latins," 185. On the ignorance of the apostles before the resurrection, see R. Latourelle, "Révélation, histoire et incarnation," *Gregorianum* 44 (1963): 257.

52. Irenaeus, *Against Heresies,* introduction 2 (PG 7:440–44); 2.27 (PG 7:802–4); 3.1.1 (PG 7:844); 3.14 (PG 7:913–14). It was all to be taught "from the housetops." H. Rahner, "The Christian Mystery and the Pagan Mystery," in *The Mysteries,* ed. Joseph Campbell (New York: Pantheon, 1955), 357–58. At least nothing important has been lost. Latourelle, "Révélation, histoire et incarnation," 258. Yet it is quite possible to publish some things while withholding others. *Gospel of Thomas* 87:10–17 (=NHL 39:10–17, p. 122); *4 Ezra* 14:6 (*OTP* 1:553).

53. So Latourelle himself, "Révélation, histoire et incarnation," 258, and A. de Bovis, "La fondation de l'Église," *Nouvelle revue théologique* 85 (1963): 12–13. Clement of Alexandria, *Stromata* 1.1 (PG 8:701), insists that his own teachings sound imbecile beside those of the apostles, as does Ignatius, *Epistle to the Trallians* 5 (PG 5:784) (long version); cf. Polycarp, *Epistle to the Philippians* 3 (PG 5:1009). Clement of Alexandria tells how early teachings inevitably become lost. *Stromatum* 1.1 (PG 8:704). Chrysostom, *In Epistolam I ad Corinthios homilia (Homily on the First Epistle to the Corinthians)* 7 (PG 61:58), and Basil, *Epistolae (Letters)* 8 (PG 32:257), note that many sacred writings have been lost. Irenaeus, *Against Heresies,* himself

puts the knowledge of the apostles in a special category, 1.13.6 (PG 7:588), and when pressed admits that the Bible does not explain everything, and so falls back on tradition, 3.3.1 (PG 7:848); when this fails him he appeals to the oldest churches, 3.4.1 (PG 7:851), and when these disagree to the most outlying ones, 3.4.2 (PG 7:855–56).

54. A favorite teaching of Basil; see Gottfried Thomasius, *Die Dogmengeschichte der alten Kirche* (Erlangen: Deichert, 1886), 279–80. The greatest teachings were not trusted to writing. *Clementine Recognitions* 1.21 (PG 1:1218); *Epistles of Paul and Seneca* 6 (*ANT,* 482); Chrysostom, *De laudibus Sancti Pauli Apostoli homilia (Homily on the Praise of St. Paul the Apostle)* 5 (PG 50:500); Chrysostom, *Homilia de Melchisedeco (Homily on Melchizedek)* 1 (PG 56:257–58).

55. Albert Schweitzer, *Geschichte der Leben-Jesu-Forschung* (Tübingen: Mohr, 1913), 1:396, admits the secrecy, though at a loss to explain it (=*The Quest of the Historical Jesus* [New York: Macmillan, 1964]). An awkward attempt to explain the secrecy of the forty days is made by Chrysostom, *Commentary on the Acts of the Apostles* 1 (PG 60:19), and borrowed by Oecumenius, *Commentary on the Acts of the Apostles* 1.2 (PG 118:45), and Theophylactus, *Exposition of the Acts of the Apostles* 1.16 (PG 125:505). On the *doctrina arcana* and the catechetical schools, see J. Baum, "Symbolic Representations of the Eucharist," in Campbell, *The Mysteries,* 261; Owen Chadwick, *From Bossuet to Newman* (Cambridge: Cambridge University Press, 1957), 68.

56. Discussed by A. Adam, "Ein vergessener Aspekt des frühchristlichen Herrenmahles," *Theologische Literaturzeitung* 88 (1963): 10–11, for Origen and Clement of Alexandria. Cf. Clement (dubia), *Homiliae (Homilies)* 19–20 (PG 2:440–41); Lactantius, *Divine Institutes* 7.26 (PL 6:815); *Clementine Recognitions* 3.74 (PG 1:1314). Baum himself is seeking to explain why representations of the Lord's supper in art are "shunned down to the fifth century." Baum, "Symbolic Representations of the Eucharist," 262.

57. Irenaeus can only use the feeble arguments of the gnostics against them: *Against Heresies* 2.2.4 (PG 7:714); 2.8.3 (PG 7:733); 2.22.6 (PG 7:785); 2.25.3 (PG 7:799); 2.8.2–3 (PG 7:804–7). "When, however, we come to inquire into the nature of this sublime knowledge, we find that it consists of subtle explanations . . . allegorical and mystical interpretations . . . and of moral precepts." John Kaye, *Ecclesiastical History of the Second and Third Centuries, Illustrated from the Writings of Tertullian* (London: Griffith, Farran and Browne, 1894), 16–17.

58. Justin, *Dialogue with Trypho* 80.2–5 (PG 6:664–65). This remains the question of questions, to distinguish Christians from pagans and true Christians from false: Augustine, *Enarrationes in Psalmos (Expositions on the Psalms)* 88 (PL 37:1134); Augustine, *Sermones (Sermons)* 109 (PL 39:1961); Augustine, *Questions from Both Sides* ("Against Pagans") 114 (PL 35:2345).

59. Irenaeus, *Against Heresies* 4.33.8 (PG 7:1077–78); Eusebius, *Ecclesiastical History* 2.1.3–4 (PG 20:136); cf. 3.32.8 (PG 20:284–86).

60. Gnosticism "left a mark upon the Christian Church which has persisted right up to the present day." Van Unnik, *Newly Discovered Gnostic Writings,* 43. Even Irenaeus's rebuttal is but "a commonplace presentation of ordinary Gnostic beliefs." A. S. Peake, quoted in Werner Förster, "Das System des Basilides," *New Testament Studies* 9 (1963): 235. The opening lines of the *Clementine Recognitions* pose the "great questions" as the legitimate object of all human search, to which, it is later explained, the gnostics had the wrong answers and Peter the right ones.

61. The charge of Irenaeus against the gnostics is not that they invent new absurdities, but that they misrepresent true and familiar doctrines; so also Polycarp, *Epistle to the Philippians* 7; Testuz, *Papyrus Bodmer X,* 52:3, p. 35. Their teachings are very convincing to Christians, for they use *genuine logia* but give them a false twist. Irenaeus, *Against Heresies,* introduction 1.1; their teachings look perfectly

orthodox, introduction 1.2; their fault is not in appealing to non-canonical writings, but in counterfeiting such, 1.20; 1.8.1; they imitate the sacrament, 1.13.2; they fake prophecy, 1.13.3–5; they counterfeit revelation with potions and drugs, 1.13.5; they parody marriage rites, 1.21.3, baptism, 1.21.3, and anointing, 1.21.4–5; they feign miraculous healings, 1.23.1. They do not (except for Marcus) change the scriptures but misinterpret them, 1.27.4; their teachings are a patchwork taken from the schools, 2.14.2–6 (see PG 7:437–754); Ignatius brings the same charges: they are bad interpreters of the good word, mixing poison with good wine. *Epistle to the Trallians* 6 (PG 5:668); as Irenaeus says, they mix chalk with milk. *Against Heresies* 3.17.4 (PG 7:931–32).

62. Such cosmic tours are described in *Jubilees, 1 Enoch, 2 Enoch, Apocalypse of Abraham, Odes of Solomon, Testament of Moses, Apocalypse of Isaiah, Ascension of Isaiah,* and *2 Baruch.* In the *Testaments of Abraham, Isaiah, Isaac, the Twelve Patriarchs, Adam,* and *Enoch,* the saint gives blessings and prophecies to his (twelve) descendants or disciples before mounting to heaven and immediately *after* his return from a cosmic tour: the parallel to the forty days is obvious; see Marinus de Jonge, *The Testaments of the XII Patriarchs* (Assen: Van Gorcum, 1953), 120.

63. Schmidt, *Gespräche Jesu,* 481–86. On the present-day "rediscovery" of the descensus, see O. Rousseau, "La descente aux enfers, fondement sotériologique du baptême chrétien," *Recherches des sciences religieuses* 40 (1951–52): 273; Martin H. Scharlemann, "He Descended into Hell," *Concordia Theological Monthly 27* (1956): 81. Bo Reicke, *The Disobedient Spirits and Christian Baptism: A Study of 1 Pet. III. 19 and Its Context* (Copenhagen: Munksgaard, 1946), 14–15, asks why the descensus is not treated in the earliest literature even though it "was clearly developed already in the writings of the Apostolic Fathers." Obviously because it was a secret teaching, though very popular in the early church. A. Dell, "Matthew 16, 17–19," *Zeitschrift für die neutestamentliche Wissenschaft* 15 (1914): 31–33.

64. For a general treatment, see John A. MacCulloch, *The Harrowing of Hell* (Edinburgh: Clark, 1930), chaps. 15 and 16. On the Jewish background, see Marc Philonenko, *Les interpolations chrétiennes des Testaments des XII Patriarches* (Paris: Presses Universitaires de France, 1960), 22–24.

65. Rousseau, "Descente aux enfers," 273–97, declares the descensus to be nothing less than "the soteriological foundation of Christian baptism," and Reicke, *Disobedient Spirits and Christian Baptism*, 245–47, notes that early Christian baptisms were consciously dramatized to represent a release from the underworld. Harris, *Odes and Psalms of Solomon*, 123, identifies Christ's own baptism with the descensus. On the baptism in the Acherusian Lake, see J. B. Frey, "La vie de l'au-dela dans les conceptions juives au temps de Jésus-Christ," *Biblica* 13 (1932): 145–46; Erik Peterson, "Die Taufe im acherusischen See," *Vigiliae christianae* 9 (1955): 1–20. Cf. John H. Bernard, "The Descent into Hades and Christian Baptism," in *Studia sacra* (London: Hodder and Stoughton, 1917), 1–50.

66. The doctrine by which "the soul mounts up continually from *topos* to *topos*" was thoroughly orthodox. Carl Schmidt, *Gnostische Schriften in koptischer Sprache aus dem Codex Brucianus* (Leipzig: Hinrichs, 1892), 193–94; Schmidt, *Gespräche Jesu*, 496–97, 512–13; cf. Origen, *Homiliae in librum Jesu Nave (Homilies on the Book of Jesus Naue)* 25 (PG 12:944); cf. *Gospel of Thomas* 90:5–7 (=NHL 42:5–7, p. 123); *Gospel of Truth* 21:23–34 (=NHL 21:23–24, p. 40); *Gospel of Philip* 133:17–18 (=NHL 85:17–18, p. 150); *Apocalypse of Paul*, in Budge, *Miscellaneous Coptic Texts*, 1027–28, 1055; Ignatius, *Epistle to the Trallians* 5 (PG 5:781–85); Ignatius, *Epistle to the Ephesians* 19 (PG 5:753); Ignatius, *Epistola ad Polycarpum (Epistle to Polycarp)* 7 (PG 5:869, calling Polycarp *theodromos*, "God runner," "Messenger of God"); *Epistle of the Apostles* 13–14; 19 (*ANT*, 489–92); *2 Enoch* 61:2; Oxyrhynchus Logion 1, 2; Clement of Alexandria, *Stromata* 2.9 (PG 8:975–81); 4.14.96 (PG 9:148–49). Cf. the doctrine of "stages of ascent," that is, three levels of enlightenment to which the Christian can aspire

even during this life. H. P. Owen, "The 'Stages of Ascent' in Hebrews 5:11–6:3," *New Testament Studies* 3 (1957): 243–53.

67. An old and orthodox idea. According to Wilhelm Bousset, *Jüdisch-christlicher Schulbetrieb in Alexandria und Rom* (Göttingen: Vandenhoeck and Ruprecht, 1915), 269, Clement of Alexandria was the first to reject it. Though it was condemned by the Council of Constantinople in 553, A. Méhat, "'Apocatastase' Origène, Clément d'Alexandrie, Acts 3, 21," *Vigiliae christianae* 10 (1956): 196, Pius XII himself in *Mediator Dei* refers to this life as "an exile."

68. Irenaeus, *Against Heresies* 1.25.4 (PG 7:676–78); *Clementine Recognitions* 2.57 (PG 1:1275). Augustine condemns the idea that the soul sinned in its premortal existence and is being punished on earth, without condemning the doctrine of premortal existence itself. M. Leusse, "Le problème de la préexistence des âmes chez Marius Victorinus Afer," *Recherches des sciences religieuses* 29 (1939): 236 n. 1, 237 n. 1. So also Cyril of Jerusalem, *Catechesis IV de decem dogmatibus (Catechetical Lecture on the Ten Doctrines)* 19 (PG 33:480); while Origen even suggests that earth life is a reward rather than a punishment. *Peri archōn (On First Things)* 1.8.4 (PG 11:179–82); 2.9.6–8 (PG 11:230–33).

69. Quote is from Barnabas, *Catholic Epistle* 21.7–8 (PG 2:780–81); cf. *Testament in Galilee* 47 (PO 9:218–19); *Gospel of Philip* 124:32–36 (=NHL 76, p. 146); *Psalms of Thomas,* in Alfred Adam, *Die Psalmen des Thomas und das Perlenlied als Zeugnisse vorchristlicher Gnosis* (Berlin: Töpelmann, 1959), 9:1, 8–10; *2 Baruch* 15:8, 16; 19:1; 21:13, 16; *Testament of Our Lord Jesus Christ* 1:13; Tertullian, *De baptismo (On Baptism)* 20.2 (PL 1:1332–34).

70. Sources listed in de Jonge, *Testaments of the XII Patriarchs,* 119–20, to which add *127 Canons of the Apostles* 2 (PO 8:575); Asin de Palacios, "Logia et Agrapha," nos. 145, 193 (PO 19:562–63, 583); *Homiliae Clementinae (Clementine Homilies)* 7 (PG 2:221); Clement, *Second Epistle to the Corinthians* 6 (PG 1:336); Ignatius, *Epistle to the*

Magnesians 5 (PG 5:761–64); Barnabas, *Catholic Epistle* 5.19–20 (PG 2:733–37); *Clementine Recognitions* 2.24 (PG 1:1261); often in 1QS *(Manual of Discipline)* III, 2–4, 13–25; IV, 1–26; cf. Psalm 1.

71. On the council, see Justin, *Dialogue with Trypho* 102 (PG 6:712–13); 141 (PG 6:797–800); *1 Enoch* 48:2–6; 62:7; Ignatius, *Epistle to the Ephesians* 19 (PG 5:753); *4 Ezra* 9:18 (*OTP* 1:545); *The Hypostasis of the Archons* 135:23–25 (=*NHL* 87:23–25, p. 153). As a genuine biblical motif, see H. Wheeler Robinson, "The Council of Yahweh," *Journal of Theological Studies* 45 (1944): 151–57; Frank M. Cross, "The Council of Yahweh in Second Isaiah," *Journal of Near Eastern Studies* 12 (1953): 274–77. Cf. N. A. Dahl, "Christ, Creation, and the Church," in William Davies and David Daube, eds., *The Background of the New Testament and Its Eschatology* (Cambridge: Cambridge University Press, 1956), ch. 22, on the importance of protology in early Christian thought; Masao Sekine, "Schöpfung und Erlösung im Buche Hiob," in *Von Ugarit nach Qumran,* ed. Johannes Hempel and Leonhard Rost (Berlin: Töpelmann, 1958), 220–21. That the Two Ways is part of the plan is specified by *Clementine Recognitions* 1.24 (PG 1:1220); 1.28 (PG 1:1222); 3.26 (PG 1:1294–95); 5.9 (PG 1:1334); cf. *Odes of Solomon* 7:11–12; 31, and Harris's comment, *Odes and Psalms of Solomon,* 129; *Apocryphon of James* 4:27–5:6 (=*NHL* 4:27–5:6, pp. 31–32); *Psalm of Thomas* 8:16–18 (the demons have a counterplan); Justin, *Dialogue with Trypho* 102 (PG 6:712–13); 141 (PG 6:797–800); and *Apologia pro Christianis (Apology)* 10 (PG 6:460–61).

72. Irenaeus calls this "the ancient law of liberty." *Against Heresies* 4.37.1–6 (PG 7:1099–1103); 4.39.3 (PG 7:1109–10). It is explained in *Clementine Recognitions* 2.23–25 (PG 1:1260–61); 3.26 (PG 1:1294); 3.49 (PG 1:1303); 3.59 (PG 1:1312); 4.24 (PG 1324); 4.34 (PG 1:1330); *Apocalypse of Paul,* in Budge, *Miscellaneous Coptic Texts,* 1066; *Testament in Galilee* 50 (PO 9:221–23); *Apocryphon of James* 4:27–5:6 (=*NHL* 4:27–5:6, pp. 31–32); Clement, *Second Epistle to the Corinthians*

7 (PG 1:337); Shepherd of Hermas, *Similitudes* 10.2 (PG 2:989); *Clementine Recognitions* 1.7–8 (PG 1:1210–11); 1.16 (PG 1:1215); 1.27 (PG 1:1222); 1.51 (PG 1:1236); 2.21 (PG 1:1259); 4.14 (PG 1:1320–21); 5.5 (PG 1:1333); *1 Enoch* 69:11; *2 Baruch* 54:15; *4 Ezra* 7:72; 8:55–56; 9:10–11 (*OTP* 1:539, 544); Tatian, *Orations* 7 (PG 6:820–21).

73. Testuz, *Papyrus Bodmer X*, 53–54, pp. 37, 39; *Psalm of Thomas* 9:7–16; *The Pearl*, in Adam, *Die Psalmen des Thomas und das Perlenlied*, 9–15; Theodosius, *On St. Michael*, in Budge, *Miscellaneous Coptic Texts*, 339–40, 906–7; *Discourse on Abbatôn*, in Budge, *Coptic Martyrdoms*, 240, 488; *Gospel of Philip* 102:29–31 (=NHL 54:29–31, p. 133); 123:4–14 (=NHL 75:4–14, p. 145); *Clementine Homilies* 9 (PG 2:241–58); Ignatius, *Epistle to the Ephesians* 13.19 (PG 5:746–47); Ignatius, *Epistle to Polycarp* 3 (PG 5:709). Satan rules the earth; see Barnabas, *Catholic Epistle* 2 (PG 2:729); 4 (PG 2:731–33); 18 (PG 2:776–77); *Psalm of Thomas* 1:17–37; 3:5–8; *1 Enoch* 6:7; 44; *2 Enoch* 18, 31:4; *Acts of Thomas* 32–33, 44–45 (*ANT*, 379–80, 386); Jerome, *Dialogue against Pelagians* 2.15 (PL 23:576–77), citing an old apocryphon. Cf. the "rule of Belial" in the Dead Sea Scrolls, Zadokite fragment 3:4; *Jubilees* 10:5–9; 11:5, etc. *On the Origin of the World* (=NHL 98:27–99:28, pp. 162–63).

74. The rules were first explained to Adam, in *2 Enoch* 30:14–15; it is the business of the true prophet to announce them. *Clementine Recognitions* 5.10 (PG 1:1334–35). The image of the games is familiar from the New Testament and the apostolic fathers, for example, Clement, *Second Epistle to the Corinthians* 7 (PG 1:337–40); and *4 Ezra* 7:57–61 (*OTP* 1:538–39). The cycle of revelation-apostasy-punishment-restoration is well known, de Jonge, *Testaments of the XII Patriarchs*, 83–86.

75. *Testament of Our Lord Jesus Christ* 1:8; 12; 13; this is a forty-day teaching, according to Adolf von Harnack, *Bruchstücke des Evangeliums und der Apokalypse des Petrus* (Leipzig: Hinrichs, 1893), 16–17. Cf. *Testament in Galilee* 7 (PO 9:184); *2 Baruch* 29, 2–3; 70:7;

Hippolytus, *On Daniel* 10 (PG 10:685); 12 (PG 10:688); *Clementine Recognitions* 5.11 (PG 1:1335). The preliminary coming is not to be confused with the later coming, A. Feuillet, "Le sens du mot parousia dans l'évangile de Matthieu," in Davies and Daube, *Background of the New Testament,* 262–69, and Guerrier, "Avant-Propos," in *Testament in Galilee* (PO 9:151).

76. Abramowski, "Der Christus der Salomooden," 60: "die Formeln eschatologisch klingen . . . aber real kultisch gemeint." Albertus F. J. Klijn, *The Acts of Thomas* (Leiden: Brill, 1962), 54–61.

77. Types of "seals" are discussed by Harris, *Odes and Psalms of Solomon,* 78–79, and Klijn, *Acts of Thomas,* 56–59. In *Odes of Solomon* 42:20, the seal is a name, in 4:8 it is a garment, in 8:16 it is a mark, in 23:8–12 it is an actual seal on a letter. In Shepherd of Hermas, *Similitudes* 8.1–2 (PG 2:971–73), all receive seals and garments; in *Similitudes* 9.16 (PG 2:995), "the seal is the water"; in *Apostolic Constitutions* 7.22 (PG 1:1012–13), it is an anointing; in Barnabas, *Catholic Epistle* 9.23–27 (PG 2:749–52), it is circumcision; in *The Pearl* it is both on a letter, 48–49, and a garment, 80–85; in the *Testament of Moses* 12:9 God wears a seal or ring on his right hand; cf. *127 Canons of the Apostles* 10 (PO 8:580). As the soul mounts up "all these stations have their *taxeis* and their seals and their mysteries." Schmidt, *Gnostische Schriften in koptischer Sprache,* 193–94. Anointing is conspicuous in the *Gospel of Philip;* there is anointing after the baptism in *Apostolic Constitutions* 7.22 (PG 1:1012–13); *Acts of Thomas* 27 (ANT, 376); 121 (ANT, 418); 132 (ANT, 422); 157–58 (ANT, 433–34); *Testament of Our Lord Jesus Christ* 2:9; *Life of Adam and Eve* 42; *2 Enoch* 21–22; 56:2; *3 Baruch* 15:1–2. The rites are often confused. Hans Achelis, *Die ältesten Quellen des orientalischen Kirchenrechtes* (Leipzig: Hinrichs, 1891), 96ff; see *OTP* 1:138 note o, and 1:677 note 15a, recommending Esther Quinn, *The Quest of Seth for the Oil of Life* (Chicago: University of Chicago Press, 1962).

78.   Without the clothing the rite is invalid, Shepherd of Hermas, *Similitudes* 9.13 (PG 2:991–94); cf. 8.2 (PG 2:977–79). The resurrection itself is conceived as the putting on of a new garment. Carl Clemen, *Primitive Christianity and Its Non-Jewish Sources* (Edinburgh: Clark, 1912), 173–74. Beside the familiar white robe of baptism, the sources speak of a garment of repentance, a skin coat worn by the prophets in the desert in the manner of John the Baptist. Robert Eisler, *Iesous basileus ou basileusas* (Heidelberg: Winter, 1929–30), 2:33–38. Clement, *First Epistle to the Corinthians* 17 (PG 1:241–44): this advice was taken literally, *Apocalypse of Peter* 17 (*ANT*, 508), where the whole community on the Mount of Transfiguration is so clothed; cf. *Ascension of Isaiah* 4:16; 11:40; and *Life of Onnophrius,* in Budge, *Coptic Martyrdoms,* 219, 469. Adam lost his garment of holiness and put on a garment of humility. Irenaeus, *Against Heresies* 3.23.5 (PG 7:963–64); *Jubilees* 3:31; while Enoch reversed the process, *2 Enoch* 22:8; cf. *Acts of Thomas* 6–7 (*ANT,* 367–68); 146 (*ANT,* 428–29); *Acts of Philip,* in Constantin von Tischendorf, *Apocalypses Apocryphae Mosis, Esdrae, Pauli* (1866; reprint, Hildesheim: Olms, 1966), 147.

79.   The meal taking place after baptism marked the death and resurrection. *Apostolic Constitutions* 8.12 (PG 1:1092–1108); Oscar Cullmann, *Urchristentum und Gottesdienst* (Zürich: Zwingli, 1950), 18, notes that this consciously goes back to "those meals where Jesus after his Resurrection appeared to the disciples." The mystic unity is emphasized in *Gospel of the Twelve Apostles* (PO 2:132–35); *Gospel of Thomas* 28:28–30 (=NHL 50:28–30, p. 129); *Gospel of Philip* 106:11–14 (=NHL 58:11–14, p. 135); *Odes of Solomon* 41:5–7; Ignatius, *Epistle to the Philadelphians* 4 (PG 5:821–28); *Didache* 9; *Testament of Our Lord Jesus Christ* 1:23, in Rahmani, *Testament of Our Lord Jesus Christ,* 44. The Jewish parallels are many, for example, "the table of the community," in 1QSa II, 18; cf. Adam, "Ein vergessener Aspekt," 9–20.

80. Aristides, *Apology* 17, 2; Minucius Felix, *Octavius* 8–10 (PL 3:266–76). The charges were "not altogether without foundation." R. M. Wilson, *The Gospel of Philip* (New York: Harper and Row, 1962), 21–22, though the nature of the rites cannot be surmised either from the anti-Christian scandal stories or from the gnostic distortions. The famous passage about the "two becoming one," etc., is not the abolition of the sexes (the later fathers often puzzle about the survival of the sexes in the resurrection), but the overcoming of all prurient distinction and rivalry, the two becoming one "in the Lord" (1 Corinthians 11:11); *Gospel of Thomas* 85: 25–35 (=*NHL* 37:25–35, p. 121); *Gospel of Philip* 113:1–26 (=*NHL* 65:1–26, p. 139); 118:13–22 (=*NHL* 70:13–22, p. 142); *Acts of Thomas* 14 (*ANT*, 370); Oxyrhynchus Frg. 655; Clement of Alexandria, *Stromata* 3.13 (PG 8:1192); 3.9 (PG 8:1165–69); Clement, *Second Epistle to the Corinthians* 12 (PG 1:345–48).

81. Robert M. Grant, "The Mystery of Marriage in the Gospel of Philip," *Vigiliae christianae* 15 (1961): 140, argues that this consisted in "literalizing" the orthodox ideas. But Irenaeus's stock charge against the gnostics is that they *de*literalize everything, their marriages of the Aeons being a good example. *Against Heresies* 1.28.1 (PG 7:690–91); 1.21.3 (PG 7:687). Tatian, *Orations* 8 (PG 6:821–25), maintains that marriage is defilement, as in the *Acts of Thomas* 12. In a conversation of the forty days Salome *wrongly* "imagined that it is wrong to have children." Clement of Alexandria, *Stromata* 3.9.66 (PG 8:1165–69).

82. While in a sense the synagogue is a shadow of the temple and preserves or rather cherishes aspects of its rites and teachings, the essential qualities of the latter are lacking in the synagogue, as indicated in Hugh W. Nibley, "Christian Envy of the Temple," in *Mormonism and Early Christianity*, 408–10, 414 (pages 110–11, 116, in this volume). The temple's "rich cosmic symbolism which was largely lost in later Israelite and Jewish tradition," William F. Albright,

Archaeology and the Religion of Israel (Baltimore: Johns Hopkins Press, 1942), 154–55, 88–89, 167, included, as Alfred Jeremias, Sigmund Mowinckel, and others have shown, such elements as its cosmic orientation, its significance as a place of contact with other worlds above and below, the ritual drama of creation, fall, and victory over death, rites of initiation and purification, etc. These basic elements of Near Eastern "patternism" have been discussed with special reference to the Jerusalem cult by the authors in Samuel H. Hooke, ed., *Myth, Ritual, and Kingship* (Oxford: Clarendon, 1958). The relation of these things to early Christian thought and practice is discussed by N. Dahl, "Christ, Creation, and the Church," 422–43. Even the Christian sacral meal which Cullmann believes was meant to supplant the temple worship, Oscar Cullmann, "Le temple de Jérusalem," *New Testament Studies* 5 (1959): 171, is now traced to the temple itself by Adam, "Ein vergessener Aspekt," 9–20. The problem of just what went on in the temple at Jerusalem at various periods calls for extensive investigation.

83. Davies, *He Ascended into Heaven*, 55. The length of the interval is not the significant thing, as van Stempvoort notes, "The Interpretation of the Ascension in Luke and Acts," 34, but its existence is.

84. Though there is a trend in the legends away from history and doctrine towards "pure thaumaturgy" (*ANT*, 474), the literature as a whole goes "back to standard themes in popular preaching and Apocryphal Acts." Klijn, *Acts of Thomas*, 25.

85. The raising of the dead is an actual demonstration of the resurrection. *Apostolic Constitutions* 5.7 (PG 1:837–52); *Letters of Severus* 88 (PO 14:153); the dead are raised in response to the challenge, "How could . . . Jesus Christ rise from the dead?" Budge, *Contendings of the Apostles*, 177–21. Upon raising a dead man, Peter cries, "Ye men of Rome, it is thus that the dead are raised up!" *Acts of Peter* 28–29 (*ANT*, 329); cf. *Gospel of the Twelve Apostles* 16 (PO 2:135); Budge, *Contendings of the Apostles*, 580–81; *Acts of Paul* ("Martyrdom") 10:1–5 (*ANT*, 294–96).

86. "I saw (Jesus) standing by thee at the moment when thou didst raise me up from the dead." Budge, *Contendings of the Apostles,* 86. "He saw our Lord Jesus Christ in the form of Judas Thomas sitting on the bed" (ibid., 343). Thecla in the arena "saw the Lord sitting, like unto Paul," in the audience, *Acts of Paul* 2:21 (*ANT,* 276). After Philip's death Jesus appears "at the end of 40 days . . . in the form of Philip" to teach his disciples. *Acts of Philip* 148 (*ANT,* 450). The post-burial appearances and the ascension of Thomas are exactly like Jesus.' *Acts of Thomas* 169 (*ANT,* 437). The closest identity is with Mary, who is inseparable from Jesus during the forty days and whose resurrection was "a greater miracle than the Resurrection of the Lord." *Gospel of the Twelve Apostles* 16 (PO 2:182). The forty days must even follow *her* resurrection! *Falling Asleep of Mary,* in Forbes Robinson, *Coptic Apocryphal Gospels* (Cambridge: Cambridge University Press, 1896), 65.

87. Jesus "would appear to them in the form in which they used to know Him," give his instructions, and then "mount up into heaven in great glory." *Story of Joseph of Arimathea* 2–3 (*ANT,* 164–65); *Acts of John* 72–76 (*ANT,* 246); *Acts of Peter* 3:1 (*ANT,* 304); 5 (*ANT,* 307–9); 16 (*ANT,* 317); 35 (*ANT,* 333); *Acts of Philip* 20 (*ANT,* 441); Budge, *Contendings of the Apostles,* 154–56, 158–62, 171, 185, 230, 247, 265–68, etc. He could appear "in any form I please" (ibid., 318); *Acts of John* 2, 4, in Montague R. James, *Apocrypha Anecdota,* 2nd series (Cambridge: Cambridge University Press, 1897), 5, 7.

88. During the feast of St. George the saint himself appeared, multiplied the loaves and wine, and brought all the sacrificed animals to life. Franz Cumont, "St. George and Mithra 'The Cattle-Thief,'" *Journal of Roman Studies* 27 (1937): 71. This multiplying of loaves and fishes is a theme of the postresurrectional meals with the Lord, for example, *Gospel of the Twelve Apostles* 2 (PO 2:132–34). Al-Thaʿlabī, *Kitāb ʿArāʾis al-majālis fī qiṣaṣ al-anbiyāʾ* (Cairo: Muṣṭafā al-Ḥalabī al-Bābī wa-Awlāduhu, 1340 A.H.), 272, 276–77, 280, cites a number of early Christian legends in which the raising of the dead is

accompanied by a feast miraculously provided from heaven. The apostles often celebrate a raising of the dead with a feast or the Eucharist. *Acts of John* 84 (*ANT,* 250); cf. *Acts of Peter* 5 (*ANT,* 308–9); *Acts of Andrew* 20 (*ANT,* 344); Budge, *Contendings of the Apostles,* 22.

89. For Victor, Budge, *Coptic Martyrdoms,* 1–101; for Theodore, Budge, *Miscellaneous Coptic Texts,* 1–48; the St. George cycle is in al-Thaʿlabī, *Kitāb qiṣaṣ al-anbiyāʾ,* 299–304; for Mercurius, Budge, *Miscellaneous Coptic Texts,* 231–99; for Sebastian, Ambrose, *Acta Sancti Sebastiani (Acts of St. Sebastian)* (PL 17:1111–50), where after his final demise the saint still returns to give instructions (PL 17:1149–50).

90. "Toutes les versions des Sept Dormants servent à prouver la résurrection des morts." Bernhard Heller, "Eléments, parallèlles et origine de la légende des Sept Dormants," *Revue des études juives* 49 (1904): 215. The identity of the Seven Sleepers with the seven heroic brothers of *4 Maccabees* 8:3–11 has long been recognized. Hippolyte Delehaye, "Hagiographie Napolitaine," *Analecta bollandiana* 57 (1939): 30. Though the latter tale is in praise of philosophy, even there the resurrection motif occurs, as when the eldest brother appears "as if he were suffering a change by fire to incorruption" (*4 Maccabees* 9:22).

91. A friend of Thecla's embraces her after one of her resuscitations crying, "Now do I believe that the dead are raised up!" *Acts of Paul* 39 (*ANT,* 280). The seven sons of Felicitas repeat the story of *4 Maccabees* 8; see Peter Chrysologus, *Sermones (Discourses)* 134 (PL 52:564–65); Gregory, *Homiliae (Homilies)* 3 (PL 76:107–8), treats the successive slayings as a repeated martyrdom of Felicitas herself. Perpetua's story is in PL 3:17–46.

92. Thomas, who is repeatedly martyred, is called the "Twin of Christ." *Acts of Thomas* 39 (*ANT,* 383–84). Philip and Paul are repeatedly executed. Budge, *Contendings of the Apostles,* 466, 470, 472, 530, and Andrew (ibid., 326–30), Mark (ibid., 258, 261–63), and Matthew (*ANT,* 460–62); when Paul survived the fire "all the people believed." Budge, *Contendings of the Apostles,* 459–60, 524.

93. Many examples may be found in L. Radermacher, "Hippolytos und Thekla: Studien zur Geschichte von Legende und Kultus," in *Sitzungsberichte der kaiserlichen Akademie der Wissenschaften in Wien, Philosophisch-historische Klasse* 182/3 (1910): 1–111; R. Vallois, "Les origines des jeux olympiques," *Revue des études anciennes* 31 (1929): 122, 128–30.

94. Arthur B. Cook, *Zeus* (Cambridge: Cambridge University Press, 1914–40), 2:417 n. 2. The seven brothers motif in notes 90 and 91 above is close to the archaic legend and cult of Niobe.

95. Puech and Quispel, "Les écrits gnostiques du Codex Jung," 15–19. The problem of such radical borrowings is treated by Erwin R. Goodenough, *Jewish Symbols in the Greco-Roman Period* (Princeton: Princeton University Press, 1953), 1:3–32.

96. See Hugh W. Nibley, "The Hierocentric State," in *The Ancient State* (Salt Lake City: Deseret Book and FARMS, 1991), 106–7, 128–31; and "The Unsolved Loyalty Problem: Our Western Heritage," in *The Ancient State,* 207–12, for references.

97. *Life of Apa Cyrus,* in Budge, *Coptic Martyrdoms,* 128–36, 381–89, is typical. Far from being unworldly, all the monkish writers in these two volumes of Budge are intrigued and bedizened by the glory of the royal court, which is constantly brought into conjunction with the heavenly court. The heroes, military or clerical, are invariably of high birth, great wealth, and brilliant popularity. Regal pomp and circumstance are not decried but described with loving enthusiasm as the earthly counterpart of the heavenly order.

98. S. MacLean Gilmour, "The Christophany to More Than 500 Brethren," *Journal of Biblical Literature* 80 (1961): 251–52, citing John Knox; and Gilmour, "Easter and Pentecost," 62–66. For some recent studies identifying these events, see Davies, *He Ascended into Heaven,* chaps. 2, 3; Grässer, "Apostelgeschichte," 155; W. von Loewenich, *Das Johannes-Verständnis im zweiten Jahrhunder*', supplement 13 of Zeitschrift für die neutestamentliche Wissenschaft

(Giessen: Töpelmann, 1932), 16; Charles E. Carlston, "Transfigura-
tion and Resurrection," *Journal of Biblical Literature* 80 (1961): 233–40;
Joachim Jeremias, "Zwischen Karfreitag und Ostern," *Zeitschrift für
die neutestamentliche Wissenschaft* 42 (1949): 194; Hans-Joachim
Schulz, "Die 'Höllenfahrt' als 'Anastasis,'" *Zeitschrift für Katholische
Theologie* 81 (1959): 1–66.

99. Justin, *Dialogue with Trypho* 2.31–34 (PG 6: 476–77); 40.4 (PG
6:561); 49.2 (PG 6:581); 52.1 and 4 (PG 6:589); 111 (PG 6:732–33);
Clementine Recognitions 1.32–33 (PG 1:1226–27); 3.61 (PG 1:1306).

100. K. Holl, "Urchristentum und Religionsgeschichte," *Zeitschrift
für systematische Theologie* 2 (1924): 403; cf. J. Jeremias, "Present
Position in the Controversy," 337–38; Schneider, "Der Beitrag der
Urgemeinde," 401–3. The argument has been skillfully pressed by C. S.
Lewis.

101. Lindeskog, "Christuskerygma und Jesustradition," 145,
149–50.

102. "Ad rudium et pauperum Apostolorum mensam, escam et
salinum vile et luteum se demittere, eis assidere, cum eis convivari."
Lapide, *Commentaria*, 17:51. On the nature of the coarse food, see
Tissot, *Life of Our Lord Jesus Christ*, 4:260.

103. So Jacques-Paul Migne, *Scripturae sacrae cursus completus*
(Paris: Migne, 1840), 23:1130; Leo, *Discourse* 73 (PL 54:394–96);
Jacquier, *Les actes des apôtres*, 9; J. Sint, "Die Auferstehung Jesu in der
Verkündigung der Urgemeinde," *Zeitschrift für katholisches Theologie*
84 (1962): 149–51.

104. Clement, *Second Epistle to the Corinthians* 5–8 (PG 1:336–41);
Didache 9; *Epistle of the Apostles* 36 (47) (*ANT*, 498); *Gospel of the
Twelve Apostles* (PO 2:154); Asin de Palacios, "Logia et Agrapha," no.
129 (PO 19:551); Justin, *Dialogue with Trypho* 110.6 (PG 6:729–32);
119.5–6 (PG 6:752–53).

105. See, for example, note 25 above.

106. Some insist that because we know the *subject* of the forty-days' discourse, we also know its *content*—which is far from being the case. Sint, "Die Auferstehung Jesu," 149–51; F. F. Bruce, *Commentary on the Book of Acts* (London: Marshall, Morgan and Scott, 1962), 34.

107. The same association of ideas meets us in such venerable documents as the so-called Shabako Stone; see Kurt Sethe, *Dramatische Texte zu altägyptischen Mysterienspielen,* vol. 10 of Untersuchungen zur Geschichte und Altertumskunde Ägyptens (Leipzig: Hinrichs, 1928), and the *Enuma Elish,* where we find the council and controversy in heaven, the creation of the world, the law of the Two Ways, the champion and redeemer of the race who overcomes the powers of death, and the obligation of the human race to participate in rites commemorating and dramatizing those cosmic events. The same motifs are conspicuous in the Dead Sea Scrolls and form the foundation of what is sometimes designated today as "patternism." Whatever the significance of these resemblances, they do show that our apocryphal concepts are *not* the contrivances of undisciplined Oriental fantasy.

108. Thus Schmidt, *Gespräche Jesu,* 205.

109. Anselm, *Homiliae (Homilies)* 7 (PL 158:628–29).

3

Christian Envy of the Temple

The Question

In his justly celebrated work on the fall of Jerusalem, S. G. F. Brandon comments on the "truly amazing" indifference of Christian writers to the importance of that event in the history of the church.[1] But if the fall of the city meant for the Christians much what it meant for the Jews, that is, "the sudden removal of the original source of authority,"[2] the loss of the temple, which was the central episode of the catastrophe, could hardly have been of less significance; yet Brandon himself, though by comparison with other scholars a positive enthusiast for the temple, minimizes its importance for the Christians as consistently as he accuses others of playing down the importance of Jerusalem.[3]

"Christian Envy of the Temple" first appeared in the *Jewish Quarterly Review* 50 (1959–60): 97–123, 229–40. The article was reprinted with the same title in *When the Lights Went Out* (Salt Lake City: Deseret Book, 1970), 55–88, and in *Mormonism and Early Christianity* (Salt Lake City: Deseret Book and FARMS, 1987), 391–434.

Why is this? Long ago Adam of St. Victor observed with wonder that the Christian fathers had always gone out of their way to avoid any discussion of the tabernacle of God, in spite of its great popular interest and its importance in the divine economy.[4] The reason for this strange attitude is, as Adam and his fellow Richard explain, that the very thing which makes the temple so attractive to many Christians, that is, the exciting possibility of a literal and tangible bond between heaven and earth, is precisely the thing that most alarms and embarrasses the churchmen.[5] Again, why so? Can it be that the destruction of the temple left a gaping void in the life of the church, a vacuum that the historians and theologians have studiously ignored, exactly as they have ignored such other appalling reverses to the church as the fall of Jerusalem and the cessation of the spiritual gifts?[6] If the loss of the temple was really a crippling blow to the church, the fact can no longer be overlooked in the interpretation of church history.

But was it such a blow? The purpose of this paper is to consider three facts that strongly support an affirmative reply, namely: (1) that many Christian writers have expressed the conviction that the church possesses no adequate substitute for the temple and have yearned for its return; (2) that determined attempts have been made from time to time to revive in the church practices peculiar to the temple; and (3) that the official Christian position, that church and temple cannot coexist and hence the latter has been abolished forever, has always been weakened by a persistent fear that the temple might be restored. These three propositions reflect in the Christian mind a sense respectively of loss, inadequacy, and misgiving. What they all share in common is envy of the temple. But before the significance of that becomes apparent, we must consider the three points in order.

Good Riddance or Tragic Loss?

Whatever the conflicting views of the earliest Christians may have been,[7] the perennial controversy regarding the temple in later times is well-illustrated by the Battle of the Books that began in the third century when Bishop Nepos attacked the "allegorists" with a book in defense of a literal and earthly millennium; in reply to this "unhealthy" teaching, Dionysius, the sophisticated Bishop of Alexandria, wrote what Jerome calls "an elegant book, deriding the old fable about the thousand years and the earthly Jerusalem with its gold and jewels, the restoration of the Temple," etc.[8] This in turn brought forth a two-volume counterblast in Jerome's day by one Apollinarius, who "not only speaks for his own following but for the greater part of the people here as well, so that I can already see," says Jerome, "what a storm of opposition is in store for me!"[9] Jerome frankly admits that the opposition represents the old Christian tradition, his own liberal "spiritualizing" interpretation running counter to the beliefs of such eminent earlier authorities as Tertullian, Victorinus, Lactantius, and Irenaeus. This puts him in a dilemma: "If we accept [the *Apocalypse of John*] literally we are judaizers, if spiritually, as they were written, we seem to be contradicting the opinions of many of the ancients."[10] From personal experience, furthermore, Jerome can tell us how the old-fashioned Christians in Jerusalem insist on pointing out the very plot of ground on the Mount of Olives "where they say the sanctuary of the Lord, that is, the Temple, is to be built, and where it will stand forever," that is, "when, as they say, the Lord comes with the heavenly Jerusalem at the end of the world."[11]

Professor Henry Cadbury, in a study in which he suggests that the earliest Christians may well have believed "that this site [the Mount of Olives] is to be the site of the *parousia*," concludes that "if other Christians, ancient and modern, have found the primitive emphasis on such a literal future event embarrassing, Luke gives no real countenance to any of their ways of avoiding it,"[12] which means that Jerome's dilemma remains unresolved to this day. Through the years the doctors have continued to dismiss a literal temple as an old wives' tale only to find all their arguments against it offset by arguments at least as potent in its favor.

First and foremost was the philosophical plea against a physical temple (supported by endless repetitions of Isaiah 66:1), that God is not to be contained in any crass material structure.[13] The fact that the invisible incorporeal God needs no visible corporeal temple was grasped "by no man at any time, either Barbarian or Greek, except by our Savior alone," writes Eusebius, forgetting in his tendentious zeal that this had been a stock theme of the schools for centuries, and that Christian Clement, speaking with the pagan voice of Alexandria, had given it his eloquent best with supporting quotations from Plato, Zeno, and Euripides.[14] The main objection to this view, however, was not its heathen coloring but the idea, pointed out later by Aquinas, that the temple was not built for God but for man, who needs a tangible image of celestial things and "special times, tabernacles, vessels, and ministers" to inculcate understanding and reverence.[15] "It cannot be too often emphasized," writes Canon Phythian-Adams, "that the belief in the Presence is not to be described as 'unspiritual' simply because Its 'tabernacle' was material." And the same scholar, who represents a surprising but unmistakable tendency to view the temple with a new sympathy and understanding, rebukes the hitherto common practice in Christian theology "of confusing a belief or doctrine with low and materialistic interpretations of it."[16] Certainly the Jews themselves were well aware of the limitations of physical buildings and needed no Greek schoolmen, levied as spokesmen for a new religion, to tell them what Solomon had said long before: "The heaven of heavens cannot contain thee, how much less this house which I have built!"[17]

Apart from its gross and earthly substance, the temple has always been criticized by the churchmen as symbolic of a narrow, selfish, tribal worldview, incompatible with the grandiose concept of a universal church.[18] Again the answer was clear: What could proclaim the oneness of God's rule and the universality of true religion more eloquently than the temple itself, "a house of prayer for all peoples," "the spiritual metropolis of all lands"?[19] Some scholars protested that the authority of the temple had been virtually abolished by the exile and the Diaspora,[20] but others pointed out with equal assurance that those misfortunes actually had the opposite effect: "Dispersion . . . increased the significance and the fascination of the Temple," while the exile "only strengthened the universal love for it."[21] Actually, the limiting of the great central rites and ordinances to one spot was the very thing that recommended the temple so strongly to the Christian schoolmen, enthralled as they were by "the withering pressure of an omnipresent and monotonous idea"—the passion for oneness.[22] Nothing on earth represented the oneness of God, his worship, and his people more perfectly than the temple had, and the church sorely missed just such a centralizing force.[23] Thus Peter Cantor in the twelfth century deplores the multiplication of Christian shrines and invites the church to "note that in all Israel there was but one Temple, one Tabernacle, one Altar," and to follow that example as "the only remedy" for "this *morbum multiplicem.*"[24]

How was such simplification to be effected? Peter and his fellows know nothing of the later device by which in theory there is only one central mass in the church "in which all the Church was thought to participate."[25] Instead he suggests a compromise that had been recommended long before: "Following the example of the *one* Temple, there should be in every city but one church, or, if it is a very large city, but a few, and those duly subordinated to the one principal church."[26] The objection to this, of course, is that the few fall as far short of the perfection of the Monad as do the many. Christian apologists had never tired of pointing out to the heathen the absurdity of their many gods and temples; how, then, were they to answer heathen and Christian criticism of the endless multiplication of Christian temples of which they first boasted[27] and which they then tried to explain away?[28]

The standard explanation was that since the church was mystically the temple, and, being universal, was *one,* it followed that the temple was still one.[29] Because Christians do all things in common, it was argued, they may be considered *as* one single temple.[30] But this was putting the cart before the horse, for, as Thomas Aquinas observes, the temple was introduced in the first place to achieve that unity—it is not the mystical result of it. But having praised the temple as the perfect expression of God's unity and of the *unitas et simplicitas* of the worship he requires, Thomas lamely adds: "But since the cult of the New Law with its spiritual sacrifice is acceptable to God, a multiplication of altars and temples is accordingly acceptable."[31] Here the word *spiritual* is expected to answer all questions and silence all objections, but Thomas's own insistence on the unique significance of the temple as a *locus electus,* a tangible center of worship for the benefit of mortal man, makes demands that abstract terminology cannot satisfy.[32] What is everywhere is nowhere, and for the very reason that God and his church *are* everywhere, there must be some special point of contact, Stephen VI is reported to have argued, around which the church might, like Israel, center its activities.[33]

Still, the idea of a spiritual temple was made to order for the schoolmen, who from the first took to it like ducks to water. The supplanting of a stone temple by "a spiritual edifice" is for August Neander nothing less than "the mightiest achievement in the history of humanity."[34] It is a simple, eloquent formula: "The Messiah's kingdom would supplant the outworn system of the past. He would raise up a new temple of the spirit."[35] "Lugeat carnalis Judaeus, sed spiritualis gaudeat Christianus!"[36] Again the argument falls flat, for the spiritual and carnal are not neatly divided between Jews and Christians, but "were to be found in both religions, and are still to be found in them."[37] If the Christian doctors knew how to spiritualize the temple, the rabbis had done a good job of de-eschatologizing long before them, and even the old-fashioned literalists knew the danger of "putting their trust in a building rather than in the God who created them."[38] In the end it was not a question of temple versus no temple but, as Irenaeus pointed out, one of proper values and emphasis.[39]

An inevitable corollary of the spiritual temple was the purely intellectual temple: *Templum Dei naturaliter est anima rationalis,* the human breast wherein "the rational and intellectual and impolluted and external unutterable nature of Divinity resides," that higher, purer temple built of abstract virtues, etc.[40] But aside from the fact that such ideas bore the trademark of the schools and were far over the heads of the general public,[41] there was no reason why an "intellectual" temple should not coexist with a real one: while the Lord referred to the temple as his body, the church, Israel, and even the dry bones of Ezekiel, Origen observes, the real temple was still standing.[42] Why not? The early fathers found "nothing absurd in saying that God's dwelling is in heaven and at the same time in the earthly Zion,"[43] and scholastic philosophers have no difficulty in viewing the temple under various mystic, moral, and material aspects without the least sense of contradiction.[44]

Along with their philosophical and moral condemnation of the temple, the doctors never tired of laboring the historical argument—the cold fact that the temple had actually been destroyed, that God had allowed its destruction and the prophets foretold it.[45] But that had happened before, following a well-established eschatological pattern which saw in the destruction itself an earnest of restoration;[46] and while in the divine plan the temple was to have its ups and downs (the Jews themselves anticipating the worst),[47] there was no doubt in the minds of Jewish and Christian "fundamentalists" that the story would end on a note of eternal triumph for the temple, whose glory was eternal, preexistent, and indestructible.[48] And if the Jews looked forward to a dark interim between the fall of the temple and the "Return and Restoration [which were an integral part of] the divine plan,"[49] so no less did the first Christians: "For the scripture says," writes one of them, "showing how the City and the Temple and the People of Israel were to be taken away, 'It shall come to pass in the last days, that the Lord will give over the sheep of his pasture, and their sheepfold and their tower to destruction.'"[50] The fathers of the fourth century were uncomfortably aware of this tradition, and Hilary states his own conviction that because of the wickedness of the times "there has for a long time been no Mountain of the Lord's House upon the earth."[51] Later churchmen are haunted by a suspicion that the church is not really the equivalent of the temple at all, but rather of the tabernacle wandering in the wilderness, while the stable and enduring temple is still to come.[52]

A favorite symbol of the transition from crass Jewish materialism to the Christian temple of the Spirit has always been the New Testament episode of the driving out of the money changers.[53] Yet how much this "obvious transfer" (as St. Leo calls it)[54] left to be desired is apparent from many a bitter comment that the church itself was as much "a den of thieves" as ever the temple was, with the obvious difference, already voiced by Origen, that "today Jesus comes no more to drive out the money-changers and save the rest!"[55] Furthermore, it has often been pointed out that the purging of the temple, far from being its death sentence, was rather a demonstration by the Lord "that he would not tolerate the slightest disrespect" for his Father's house.[56]

In the same way, the other classic scriptural arguments against the temple have either backfired or proven highly equivocal. The famous prophecy that not one stone should remain upon another, hailed by the churchmen as a guarantee of eternal dissolution,[57] contains nothing to confirm or deny a future restoration, and may well have been spoken "with the sorrow of a patriot rather than the wrath of an iconoclast."[58] If the rending of the veil has been treated as a symbol of irreversible eradication,[59] it has suggested with equal force a broadening and expanding of revelation.[60] Jesus' invitation to "destroy this temple" and his conditioned promise to rebuild the same are often taken—but only by a liberal revamping of the text—to mean the opposite, namely, that he will destroy the temple himself, and instead of rebuilding it bring something totally different in its place: "'Finish then,' he might have implied, 'this work of dissolution: in three days will I . . . restore . . . not a material Temple, but a living Church.'" Dean Farrar's interpretation is typical, resting as it does not on what Jesus said but on what "he might have implied."[61]

... Tamen usque recurret

The temple was driven out with a fork by Jerome and his intellectual friends. On one thing all the spiritual children of Alexandria—Greek, Jewish, Christian, and Muslim—have always seen eye to eye, and that is the conviction that the old eschatology with its naive literalism and its millennial temple was unworthy of thinking men, "repugnant to every principle of faith as well as reason."[62] Of these intellectuals none have been more dedicated to the party line than the Christian schoolmen, whose opinions inevitably became the official doctrine of a church which drew its leaders almost exclusively from their ranks. Yet they were not the only force to be reckoned with, and by the time "St. Augustine's *City of God* had come to replace millenarianism as the official doctrine of the church,"[63] the more tangible and sensuous aspects of the temple, enhanced by time and legend, were exercising their powerful attraction on two highly susceptible and influential bodies—a spectacle-hungry public and a power-hungry government.

As to the first of these, it is apparent from Jerome's experience that a large part of the Christian society did not lose sight of the temple after its destruction but spoke longingly of its return. Students today are more inclined than they have been in the past to concede to the temple a high place in the estimation of Jesus,[64] of the prophets before him,[65] and of the apostles and the church after him.[66] "The ethical monotheism of the Wellhausen era," that made short work of the temple and its ritualism, now yields to recognition of the importance of the ritual drama of the temple not only as "a basic component of Israel's religion," but of early Christianity as well.[67] For both, the way to heaven led through the temple, and if that was but an intermediate step in the salvation of the race, it was nonetheless an indispensable one.[68] It was all very well for the orators of the fourth century to declaim that in the church "the goal of all old Testament hopes had now come," that "the religion of promise and pilgrimage" had given way to "one of achievement and fulfilment"—the simpler Christians knew better: "Christians have not yet attained their goal; they too must run their course (Hebrews 12:1)."[69] The Christian still needed the temple and always remained a pilgrim to Jerusalem in a very literal sense. Even the learned doctors of the second and third centuries "were unable to resist the fascination of the holy places" and came with the rest to see the spot where the Lord had left the earth and where he would return to his temple.[70] In vain did the great fathers of the following centuries protest against the silly custom, clearly pointing out that it was in direct conflict with the official doctrine of the spiritual temple: the pilgrimage went right on.[71]

The Emperor Constantine's plan "to legislate the millennium in a generation" called for the uniting of the human race in the bonds of a single religion, under a single holy ruler, administered from a single holy center.[72] It was the old "hierocentric" concept of the sacral state, represented among others by the *Roma aeterna* of which Christian Rome claimed to be the revival,[73] but also typified from time immemorial in the temples of the East, each a scale model of the cosmos, which was thought literally to revolve around it.[74] Constantine's architectural projects proclaim his familiarity with the idea of a *templum mundi* as a physical center of the universe,[75] just as clearly as his panegyrists hail him in the role of Solomon the temple builder.[76] "It is our most peaceful Solomon who built this Temple," cries the orator at the dedication of one of Constantine's vast "cosmic" rotundas, "and the latter glory of this House is greater than the former." Just as Christ transferred "from sordid flesh to a glorified body," so the church now has a much more glorified body than before.[77] Let no one mistake this for the incorporeal temple of the doctors, who protested briefly and ineffectively against all this materialism;[78] this really fulfills the prophecy (Haggai 2:9), no longer in words only but in deeds.[79] The same rhetorical license that had vaporized the temple of Jerusalem by its appeal to higher things was not employed to justify its very solid successors, and before a rapt audience the great Christian orator could convert a monster pile, window by window and stone by stone, "into a spiritual temple structure" by the bewitching power of allegory.[80]

Immediately after his return from the Council of Nicea, Bishop Macarius of Jerusalem, by authorization of the emperor, demolished the temple of Jupiter that the Romans had "built on the very spot where formerly the Temple of God had stood," and in the process discovered the crypts of the Cross and the Holy Sepulchre, "and," Eusebius significantly adds, "the Holy of Holies crypt," which was identical in form with the latter.[81] Over the holy spot the emperor or his mother had built the wonderful structure which they called "the New Jerusalem, having erected it in the place of the ancient one that had been abandoned," the Holy Sepulchre serving as the pivot and center of the whole sacred complex.[82] The temple complex was supplanted by Christian buildings. Theodoret pointedly compares the Churches of the Crucifixion, Resurrection, and Ascension with the ruined temple and asks how the Jews in the face of that can have the effrontery even to remain in the city: "The Babylonians never came to worship at *their* Temple," he argues, "while all the world flocks to our churches," thus proving that the true house of God that draws all nations to Jerusalem is not their temple but our church.[83] Chrysostom draws a like conclusion as he ecstatically views those vast panegyrises, those gorgeous year-assemblies at the shrine of the martyrs that represent the brilliant wedding of Christianity with the ever-popular pagan cults with their feasts and markets at holy tombs: "What does this all mean?" he asks, and the answer is clear: "It means that the Temple has been abolished."[84] We don't need to go to Jerusalem anymore, John assures his people, just as his friend Gregory of Nyssa can announce that the church can "supplant the faded antique glory of our cities by our own Christian glory."[85]

Of the many duplicates of Constantine's New Jerusalem the most ambitious was Justinian's "mighty glorious Temple, the Temple of my Lord, a heaven here below which I ween amazes even the reverencing Seraphim. If God should ever condescend to abide in a house made with hands," the panegyrist continues, "this surely is the House!"[86] As a crowning gesture, the emperor had fetched from Carthage the very vessels that the Roman soldiers had plundered from the temple of Jerusalem long before. But then in an even more significant gesture, the haughty Justinian for the only time in his life heeded the advice of the hated Jews and in superstitious dread ordered the vessels returned "in haste to Jerusalem, where he had them deposited in a church."[87] It was all very well to set up a new and holier Rome on the Bosphorus, but when it came to a showdown not even a Justinian dared to arrogate the authority of the house of God at Jerusalem.[88]

The man who dared most was Pope Leo. Behind him he had the tradition of the empire, now Christian, with Rome "holy among cities" as the center of the world.[89] But how could the church have two centers? The churchmen displayed considerable ingenuity in their arguments to show how a large number of churches could carry on the tradition of a single temple,[90] but by the time of Constantine it was recognized that if there was ever to be peace in the church what was needed

was not a vague universality and equality, but a highly central-
ized authority.[91] Leo, who did more than any other man to
transform the old universal *devotio Romana* into a new *devotio
Christiana*,[92] clearly saw in the temple at Jerusalem his most serious opponent.[93] His sermons bristle with barbed and invidious remarks that betray his touchiness on the subject. In Leo's
Rome, as Michael Seidlmayer puts it, "die christliche Kirche
steht auf dem Fundament des heidnischen Tempels."[94] Leo explains this away by appealing to the well-established Roman
doctrine of *renovatio* with a new twist: Rome has died pagan
and been resurrected Christian.[95] The tomb of Peter now performs the function that once belonged to the *templum* of Hadrian, the great round tomb by the Tiber that was designed to
draw all the world to it, while Hadrian's image now stands in
the temple of Jerusalem—the roles of the two cities have been
neatly reversed.[96]

Leo freely admits the debt of Christian Rome to pagan
Rome[97] and sees in the great Easter and Christmas congrega-
tions of his people both the old Roman national assembly and
the gathering of Israel at the temple: "Here you see the heavenly Jerusalem, built of all nations," he cries, addressing such
assemblies, "purged of all impurity on this day, it has become
as the Temple of God!"[98] "Now a new and indestructible
Temple has been erected," with Leo himself presiding in it, or-
dained in honor of Christ, the prophet "after the order of
Melchizedek, . . . not after the order of Aaron whose priesthood
. . . ceased with the Law of the Old Testament."[99] Rome has not
abolished the rites of the temple, however, but simply taken
them over, every particle of the ancient ordinances and imagery having been absorbed in the Christian sacraments: "Ours
today is the circumcision, the anointing of priests, etc. . . . Ours
is the honor of the Temple!"[100] Thanks to the ministrations of

Peter and Paul, the people of Rome are now "a holy generation, a chosen people, a priestly and royal city." In a word, Rome was now Jerusalem.[101]

But Leo protests too much. His Easter sermons, like Hilary's *Tract on the Psalms,* Ambrose's *De Sacramentis,* Jerome's letters from Bethlehem, and Chrysostom's great work on the priesthood, breathe less of pious conviction than of envy. The first of these displays a positive phobia of a literal temple, against which it wages truceless war.[102] "We admire the mysteries of the Jews, given to our fathers, first for their antiquity, and then for their sanctity," says Ambrose, reassuring his followers, "But I can promise you that the Christian sacraments are both holier and older." For the former rites go back only to Moses, while Melchizedek is the author of the latter. *Quis est Melchisedek?* Who but the Justice, Peace, and Wisdom of God—is there anything more timeless or holy than a pure abstraction?[103] Jerome, explaining to a friend that the temple was always exclusively reserved to the Christians, concedes that the holy of holies was a wondrous thing, and promptly adds: "But doesn't the Sepulchre of the Lord appear more worshipful to you? As often as we enter it we see the Lord lying there . . . and the Angel sitting at his feet."[104] Chrysostom, constantly approached by disillusioned Christians wanting to know what has happened to the ancient glories of Israel, is able to reply with stirring rhetoric: In ancient times only Moses could approach God, but now we all see him face to face. Moses feared God—but no one fears him today. Israel heard the thunder and trembled—we hear God's actual voice and are not afraid.[105] We have angels all around us in the church today—you can see them if only you will open your mental eyes.[106] The priest ministering at our altar is a more awesome object than the high priest in the temple, since "he casts aside all carnal thought and like a disembodied spirit views celestial things by pure mind alone."[107] The Jewish temple was a mere shadow, the churchmen repeat: *we* have the real thing. "They had the Tabernacle, *we* see Truth face to face!"[108] Do we? Yes, indeed, "but in a higher and hidden sense."[109]

Leo's imagery manifests an awareness that in snubbing the temple the church would be missing a good thing. Actually the fathers of the preceding generation had fumbled the ball badly when they threw out the temple. But before the church could recover, a new and formidable player, Islam, had snatched it up and run the whole length of the field.

When Omar conquered and entered Jerusalem in A.D. 638 he asked first of all to be shown "the glorious Temple that Solomon had built," only to discover that the Christians had converted the place into a garbage dump.[110] The treasure that the churchmen had so foolishly thrown away the Muslims were quick to exploit, promptly rebuilding the temple and restoring it to its prestige as a center of world pilgrimage.[111] They had already harnessed its unique powers by "transferring to Mecca cosmological ideas in vogue among Jews and Christians concerning the sanctuary of Jerusalem,"[112] and though the legends of the Kaaba, of its founding and refounding by Adam and Abraham as an earthly replica of the eternal preexistent heavenly prototype, etc., were borrowed freely from Jerusalem, there is no long history of bitter rivalry between the two.[113] For Islam, Jerusalem remained par excellence the City of the Holy House, and as late as the eleventh century anyone who could not make the hajj to Mecca was instructed to go to the great feast at Jerusalem instead.[114] The Muslim intellectuals, exactly as the Jewish and Christian doctors before them, protested against the glorification of a mere building, and campaigned vigorously against the pilgrimages,[115] but the temple had a powerful advocate in Christian jealousy. Like children fighting for a toy, each faction came to prize the temple more highly when it saw how much the other wanted it.

This jealous rivalry became apparent on the very day Omar entered Jerusalem and visited the temple ruins "in all humility and simplicity." The Christians, who saw in his unassuming manner "only a Satanic hypocrisy," were piously horrified at the sight, and the Patriarch Sophronius cried out: "This, surely, is the Abomination of Desolation in the Temple, of which David [*sic*] prophesied."[116] For the Christians it was *their* temple now, though they had turned it into a dung heap.[117] Such horror the Jews of old had expressed at the sight of profane feet in the temple, and presently the Muslims took up the refrain, banishing Christians and Jews on pain of death from the sacred precincts "where the Saracens believe, according to their law, that their prayers are more readily answered than anywhere else."[118] The only genuine religious clashes between Christians and Muslims, Friedrich Müller informs us of the Crusades, were the two fights for the temple, when the Christians took it in 1099 and the Muslims got it back in 1187—"und damit war die Geschichte des Glaubenskrieges als solches ziemlich aus."[119] Solomon's temple was in each case, as it had been in Jewish times, the last redoubt; there alone neither side gave or asked for quarter; it was the ultimate all-out objective, and each conqueror in turn entered the holy place with songs of apocalyptic joy.[120]

Actually the possession of the temple complex was more than a mere matter of prestige. In the endless rivalries of the Christian sects there was just one claim to supreme authority that could neither be duplicated nor matched: "Those who cannot be reached by scriptural and doctrinal arguments," says a writing attributed to Athanasius, are bound to credit the claims of that church which holds the holy places, including

"Zion, where the salvation of the world was worked out. . . . And if the opposition say that we hold those places by the brute force of imperial arms, let them know that . . . Christ has never allowed His Places to fall into the hands of heretics." It was a strong argument until Islam took over.[121]

From the fourth century on, Christians were taught to view the Holy Sepulchre rather than the temple as the religious center of the universe. But in supplanting the temple its Christian counterpart could never escape the claims and traditions of its predecessors—in Jerusalem the pilgrim was never out of the shadow of the temple, as is strikingly illustrated in the Lady Aetheria's (Silvia's) full description of the Easter celebration at Jerusalem at the end of the fourth century.

According to Aetheria, the great culmination of the pilgrimage was the *dies enceniarum* commemorating the dedication of the great Churches of the Cross and the Holy Sepulchre *and* of the Temple of Solomon. The supreme consummation and fulfillment of all the pilgrim's toil and yearning, as the lady describes it, was that moment when he was permitted to come forward and kiss the true Cross on Golgotha, "*at the same time* kissing the ring of Solomon and the horn with which the kings of Israel were anointed."[122] Again, the great annual sermon attended by all the clergy and the pilgrims, the only universal compulsory assembly, had to be delivered "always in that place . . . to which on the 40th day Joseph and Mary brought the Lord in the Temple."[123] Silvia's pilgrim is never allowed to forget that he is a pilgrim to the temple.[124] Indeed, whatever was holy about the Holy City was made such by contact with the temple, which, as Photius observes, "has the power to sanctify other things . . . a sort of divine grace to make holy."[125] Thus "the temple consecrated the city" and progressively sanctified the holy mountain, the Holy City, the Holy Land, and ultimately the whole earth;[126] "the Eternal Presence renders the new Jerusalem one vast *naos*," where John saw no temple, not because there was none, but because it was all temple.[127]

In the reports of both Eastern and Western travelers the various holy places of the temple complex are constantly confused and identified with each other.[128] Especially common is the locating of the Holy Sepulchre, the holy of holies, and the Cross of Golgotha (directly over the skull of Adam) at one and the same spot.[129] In old maps and drawings the temple and the Holy Sepulchre are depicted alike, as a circular structure marking the exact center of the earth, with its four shrines marking the points of the compass. The two are virtually identical.[130]

Upon taking Jerusalem in 1099 the Crusaders moved straight to the object of their desire, the Holy Sepulchre, and then proceeded directly to Solomon's temple: *ad dominicum sepulcrum, dehinc etiam ad Templum.*[131] As they marched they sang apocalyptic hymns of joy hailing the millennial day and the New Jerusalem.[132] The Crusades are a reminder that Christianity was never able to settle for a spiritual temple or forget the old one: "It is foolish and unmeet," writes an indignant churchman, "for Fulcher to distort utterances applying to the spiritual reign and to spiritual things in such a way as to make them apply to buildings or earthly localities, which mean nothing at all to God." But Fulcher knew what he was doing: "at the time," our critic confesses, "everybody was sunk in the error of that kind of gross darkness, clergy and laity, learned and military alike."[133] To explain away the disturbing veneration of the Crusaders for the temple, scholars have argued that they were really confusing it with the Holy Sepulchre;[134] but they could hardly have confused the most sacred object on earth with anything but another very sacred object, and it is absurd to suppose that when they spoke of the Temple of Solomon they had no idea of what they were talking about.[135] Typical of modern prejudice is the naive insistence that the Knights Templars took their singular title from their street address, their headquarters being by the merest coincidence near the site of Solomon's temple. But if the title *Pauperes commilitione Christi templique Salomoniaci* means anything, it means that these gentlemen fought for Christ *and* the Temple of Solomon, and were perfectly aware that the institution of the pilgrimage, which it was their special office to render secure, went back to the days of the temple.[136]

Though freely admitting the liturgical indebtedness of the church to the synagogue, students of ritual and liturgy have displayed singular reluctance to concede anything at all to the temple.[137] Yet if the church of the fourth and fifth centuries, while embracing popular heathen cult practices everywhere, also aped the synagogue with a zeal that was almost comical,[138] we must not forget that "the worship of the early Synagogue was based on the Temple liturgy."[139] Nay, the fathers, early and late, derive Christian worship directly from the temple, though like Hilary they may make a hair-splitting distinction between Jewish worship *in templo* and Christian worship *ad templum.*[140] They boast that the church possesses all the physical properties of the temple—the oil, the myrrh, the altar, and incense, hymns, priestly robes, etc., everything, in fact, but the temple itself, for "in the place of the tangible Temple we behold the spiritual."[141] Strange, that the solid walls should vanish and all the rest remain! Even the unleavened bread was retained in the West as an acknowledged heritage of the temple, in spite of the much more appropriate spiritual symbolism of the leavened bread preferred by the Eastern churches, "for we do not reject all the practices of the Old Law," says Rupert in explaining this, "We still offer incense . . . daily, the holy oil of anointing is among us, we have bells in the place of ancient trumpets, and many suchlike things."[142] So we find "veils of the Temple" in Christian churches,[143] inner shrines called tabernacles, awesome holies of holies entered only by prince and patriarch for the year-rite,[144] buildings and altars oriented like synagogues— which imitated the temple in that respect,[145] dedication rites faithfully reproducing those of Solomon's temple,[146] and a body of hymns "so obviously sung in the Temple that there is no need for any words to prove this."[147] In ritual texts priests are regularly referred to as Levites, and the bishop, though his office and title derive from the synagogue and not the temple, is equated with Aaron the high priest. Rabanus Maurus leaves us in no doubt of what his people were thinking when they hailed their fine church with *templum Domini, templum Domini, templum Domini est!*[148]

The Dread and Envy of Them All

Though it did not need to be pointed out to them, the Jews were ever reminded by Christian theologians that without their temple they were helpless.[149] On the other hand, the churchmen recognized with a shudder that if they ever got their temple back again the same Jews would be very dangerous indeed. "*If the Jews had* [their ancient institutions]," Athanasius observes, "then they could deny that Christ had come . . . ; but now all prophecy is sealed, and their gift of prophecy, their holy city, and their Temple are taken away—forever."[150]

That ringing "forever" is the key to the whole problem. The joy of the clergy, some of whom take genuine pleasure in reporting every fresh disaster and indignity to the temple, would be cold comfort indeed were this Banquo ever to rise and push them from their stools. The most disturbing aspect of the temple was the apocalyptic assurance of its restoration, and every device of rhetoric and logic (in the absence of a single verse of scripture to support the thesis and a great many to refute it) was employed to convince the world that the prophetic "forever" applied not to the *restoration* of the temple, but to its *destruction*.[151] The strongest argument was the historical one, the case stated by Hippolytus, that since the temple *has* never been restored it should be plain to all "by now" that it never *will* be. The greatest comfort Origen can muster for the future is the fact that in his day the temple cult had been interrupted for a longer period than ever before. True, the suspended rites have always been resumed in the past, but in this case enough time has passed to warrant one in being so bold as to express an opinion that they will *never* be restored.[152] Later theologians built the feeble argument into their chief bulwark against the temple, Chrysostom reinforcing it with the observation that while Josephus describes the destruction of the temple, he has nothing to say of its restoration, which proves "that he did not dare predict that it would be restored again," which in turn proves that it never can be![153] Actually "the remorseless logic of history," far from "confuting" early Christian hopes for the temple,[154] has seriously confuted the opposition, whose program has always called for a complete transfer of the ancient heritage to the new church, a transfer which "the continued existence of the Jewish nation and cult" has rendered desperately overdue.[155]

How touchy an issue the temple has always been is shown clearly enough by the extreme reluctance of the churchmen to talk about it. Anything that even reminds them of it seems to rub them on a raw place. The mere sight of its ruins, instead of providing the eyes of the monks of Palestine with a gratifying spectacle and an edifying object lesson as the pagan ruins did, drove them wild with fury—"a detestable thing that causes appallment to the worshippers of Christ."[156] The Jews had to pay a heavy tariff for the luxury of mourning at those ruins, for their mourning was not only a reminder of what the temple *had* been, but also of what it *would* be.[157] No wonder the exasperated fathers ask the Jews why they insist on hanging around Jerusalem after their temple has been destroyed, and bid them take the hint and be gone: "Everything you treasured in Jerusalem now lies in ruins, and your world-renowned temple is now the city dump of a town called Aelia."[158] On the other hand, Theophylactus reports that people even in his day tried to prove from the presence of ruins on the holy mount "that Christ was a liar."[159]

This last point, and the fundamental insecurity which underlay it, is illustrated by one of the most dramatic Christian legends, in which the mere report of the Emperor Julian's intention to assist in rebuilding the temple was magnified into the greatest crime, and its failure into the greatest miracle, of postapostolic history.[160] The story begins with the Jews announcing to the monarch that they are paralyzed without their temple: "We cannot worship without it."[161] The wily emperor sees that the Christians will be equally paralyzed by its restoration, and plans in the rebuilding of the temple to deliver the *coup de grâce* to Christianity by demonstrating once and for all that Jesus was a false prophet.[162] For the Christians the whole issue of the truth and survival of their religion hinges on the rebuilding of the temple. To make this clear to all, the bishop of Jerusalem, we are told, had gone about preaching that in Daniel and the Gospels the Lord had predicted that the Jews would never, to the end of time, be able to place one stone of the temple upon another.[163] Since the bishop (whose extensive writings make no mention of our story) preached no such thing,[164] since no such prophecy exists in the scriptures, and since the restoration of the temple would not confute a single recorded utterance of Jesus, it is plain that the churchmen themselves have chosen to make an issue of the temple and thereby rendered coexistence of church and temple impossible.[165] In this case only one solution was possible: a succession of stunning and theatrical miracles in the best fourth-century tradition (but also of a type of miracle story that had been growing up around the temple for many centuries)[166] frustrated the evil project at every step. Day after day the stubborn Jews persisted, and day after day great balls of fire chased them all over the temple rock, consuming them like flies, while the earth shook and the heavens gave forth with a succession of superspectacular displays. Among all the conflicting accounts, Michael Adler had no difficulty finding the most probable source of the legends, which grow like a snowball;[167] yet to this day Christian scholars cite the fantastic and contradictory stories not only as actual fact, but also as positive proof that Jerusalem and the temple can never be restored.[168]

When Athanasius assures us that no crime can be more monstrous than that of converting a church into a synagogue, he makes it clear that that is not because one poor synagogue more or less makes so much difference, but because such a gesture "prepares the way" for the sitting of the antichrist in the temple.[169] The antichrist-in-the-temple prophecy has always cast a dark shadow over the pages of the fathers, and though most of them prefer an allegorical interpretation, a large and influential number of them insist on taking the thing literally, however terrible the prospect. It is *definitive templum Dei,* whether we like it or not, they assure us, and before the adversary can usurp his place in the temple, that temple must be rebuilt.[170]

Church writers have done their best to brighten the gloomy picture. They have reassured us that the only really *literal* aspect of the temple was its destruction;[171] they have told comforting stories of frustrated attempts to rebuild it;[172] they report with a great sigh of relief the collapse of the Montanist project for re-building the New Jerusalem;[173] and, as we have seen, they taxed the resources of exegesis to discover a ray of hope in the scrip-tures. Yet all this but betrays rather than allays their misgivings: towards the Jews and their temple, their words and deeds remain those of men haunted by a sense of insecurity.[174] Why otherwise would they forbid the Jews even to imitate the architecture of the temple in their synagogues?[175] The intellectuals who liqui-dated the temple once and for all in the economy of the church fondly supposed that their own eloquence could more than take its place: while the emperors have taken upon themselves the expense and responsibility of erecting the physical edifice, Jerome assures us, it is *eloquentia* that warrants the tabernacling of the Spirit therein.[176] If the temple of the Spirit was built with-out hands, human tongues worked overtime on the project, and the finished structure remains a typically unconvincing pro-duction of the Age of Rhetoric.[177]

The Reformation as a reaction against ritualism could hardly be expected to capitalize on the Christian need for the temple or its equivalent, and indeed leading Protestant schol-ars confess that vagueness and uncertainty in ritual matters was perhaps the most serious defect in the work of the Reformers.[178] Yet the Protestant experience seems simply to be repeating the cycle, for we have seen how the doctors of an-cient times condemned the temple and its rites with overhasty zeal, and how their successors, seeking like Esau to mend the damage and "inherit the blessing" when it was all too late, in-troduced into the vacuum a botched and hybrid ritual. It was the pagan element in that ritual which the Reformers found so objectionable and exposed so skillfully.[179] Neither group has grounds for complacency, and it would be hard to determine which of the two condemns the temple with greater vigor.

By loosely and inaccurately equating the temple with the synagogue, it has been possible for Christian scholars in the past to claim victory for the church without the painful necessity of mentioning the temple too much or even at all, the assumption being that the church's triumph over the synagogue answereth all things.[180] But with the current emphasis on eschatology and ritual, the temple can no longer be kept in the background. *Eschatologie hat über uns keine Macht mehr!* has been the common creed of the clergy,[181] but eschatology now returns like an unwelcome ghost, and with it comes the temple. So while some Christian scholars still denounce the temple with surprising vehemence,[182] others are markedly hesitant,[183] and still others have reached the point of unabashedly accepting "the literalness of the future temple and its sacrificial system."[184] All three of these attitudes bespeak a sense of insecurity and inadequacy.

The moral of our tale is that the Christian world has been perennially haunted by the ghost of the temple—a ghost in which it does not believe. If the least be said for it, the temple has never lost its power to stir men's imaginations and excite their emotions, and the emotion which it has most often inspired in Christian breasts has certainly been that of envy, a passion the more dangerous for being suppressed. The temple has cast a shadow over the claims and the confidence of the Christian church from early times, a shadow which is by no means diminishing in our own day. If we seem to have labored the obvious in pointing this out, it is only because the obvious has been so long and so resolutely denied or ignored in high places.

Notes

1. Samuel G. F. Brandon, *The Fall of Jerusalem and the Christian Church* (London: Society for the Promotion of Christian Knowledge, 1951), 10–11.

2. Ibid., 250.

3. While opposing the usual tendency to minimize the temple in the economy of the early church, for example, ibid., 29, 39, 164–65, 263, Brandon bestows upon the city of Jerusalem the laurels that rightfully belong to the temple, for example, 19–21.

4. "Mirum est quod quase hunc locum ita praetergressi sint." Adam Praemonstratensis (Adam of St. Victor), *De tripartito tabernaculo (On the Tripartite Tabernacle)* 2 (PL 198:625). Richard of St. Victor writes on the same subject by popular demand—"rogatus ab amicis," in *De tabernaculo (On the Tabernacle)* 1 (PL 196:211–12).

5. Adam of St. Victor, *On the Tripartite Tabernacle* 2 (PL 198:625); Richard of St. Victor, *On the Tabernacle* 1 (PL 196:211–12), and 2 (PL 196:223–42; cf. PL 196:306).

6. Of the latter calamity Bishop John Kaye writes: "The silence of ecclesiastical history respecting the cessation . . . is to be ascribed . . . to the combined operation of prejudice and policy—of prejudice which made them reluctant to believe, of policy which made them anxious to conceal the truth." John Kaye, *Ecclesiastical History of the Second and Third Centuries, Illustrated from the Writings of Tertullian* (London: Griffith Farran, 1894), 50.

7. Discussed by Brandon, *Fall of Jerusalem*, 39, 127, 262–64. See note 66 below.

8. Eusebius, *Historica ecclesiastica (Ecclesiastical History)* 7.24.1–9 (PG 20:692–96), quoting Dionysius at length. Jerome, *Commentarius in Isaiam prophetam (Commentary on Isaiah)* 18 (PL 24:627).

9. "Quem non solum suae sectae homines, sed et nostrorum in hac parte dumtaxat plurima sequitur multitudo, ut praesaga mente jam cernam quantorum in me rabies concitanda sit." Jerome, *Commentary on Isaiah* 18 (PL 24:627).

10. Jerome, *Commentary on Isaiah* 18 (PL 24:627). The case for the literalists is stated by Cyril of Jerusalem, who insists that Jesus meant the real temple when he spoke of his Father's house: "Tōi Christōi peisthēsometha tōi legonti peri tou hierou [i.e., Luke 2:49; John 2:16] . . . di' hōn saphestata ton en Hierosolymois proteron naon oikon einai tou heautou Patros hōmologei." *Catechesis VII. de Patre (Catechetical Lecture on the Father)* 6 (PG 33:612).

11. Jerome, *Commentary on Jeremiah* 31.38 (PL 24:920): "Judaei videlicet et nostri Judaizantes, conantur ostendere . . . ibi dicunt sanctuarium Domini, id est templum esse condendum, mansurumque in perpetuum," etc.; cf. Jerome, *Commentary on Isaiah* 15.54 (PL 24:516).

12. Henry J. Cadbury, "Acts and Eschatology," in *The Background of the New Testament and Its Eschatology,* ed. William D. Davies and David Daube (Cambridge: Cambridge University Press, 1956), 309, 316.

13. Therefore even Solomon's temple was "neque legitimum neque devotum," according to Zeno, *Tractatus (Tractate)* 1.14 (PL 11:355), since God "reprobat . . . tam immensum, tam insigne, tam opulens templum," etc., ibid. (PL 11:356–58). The same argument is used by Hilary, *Tractatus super Psalmos (Treatise on the Psalms)* 126 (PL 9:694–99); Lactantius, *Divinae institutiones (Divine Institutes)* 6.25 (PL 6:728–32); Isidore, *Epistolae (Letters)* 4.70 (PG 78:1132–33); cf. 1.20 (PG 78:196), and 1.196 (PG 78:356); Procopius, *Commentarius in Isaiam (Commentary on Isaiah)* 6.5 (PG 87:1937).

14. Eusebius, *Praeparatio evangelica (Preparation for the Gospel)* 3.13–17 (PG 21:220–28); Clement of Alexandria, *Stromata* 5.11 (PG 9:112–16); 7.5 (PG 9:436–40). Theodoret, *Graecarum affectionum*

curatio sermo (Sermon on the Treatment of Greek Illnesses) 3 (PG 83:885), quotes Zeno and Plato in this connection.

15. Thomas Aquinas, *Summa theologica* 1a2æ, 102.4; Dominican ed., 29:152–77.

16. William J. Phythian-Adams, *The People and the Presence* (London: Oxford University Press, 1942), 60.

17. 2 Chronicles 6:18.

18. So Irenaeus, *Contra haereses (Against Heresies)* 4.34.4 (PG 7:1085–86); Hilary, *Treatise on the Psalms* 118.4 (PL 9:643); Lactantius, *Divine Institutes* 4.14 (PL 6:1021–22); Chrysostom, *De sancta Pentecoste homilia (Homily on the Holy Pentecost)* 1.1 (PG 50:453), etc. This was a favorite theme with the moderns who feel that the liquidation of the temple was indispensable to "the absolution of God's worship from all bonds of time and nationality." Bernhard Weiss, *The Life of Christ,* trans. John W. Hope (Edinburgh: Clark, 1883–84), 3:261.

19. Jacob S. Raisin, *Gentile Reactions to Jewish Ideals* (New York: Philosophical Library, 1953), 225; cf. 15–16, 34, 94.

20. So Ernest Renan, *Antichrist* (Boston: Roberts, 1897), 187–88; Arthur S. Peake, ed., *The People and the Book* (Oxford: Clarendon, 1925), 281.

21. Quotations are, respectively, from Andrew M. Fairbairn, *Philosophy of the Christian Religion* (New York: Macmillan, 1902), 487, and Albert T. Olmstead, *Jesus in the Light of History* (New York: Scribner's Sons, 1942), 69–70; cf. Stanley A. Cook, *The Old Testament* (New York: Macmillan, 1936), 130.

22. Quotation from John B. Bury. From early times Christians debated the cosmic significance of the oneness of the temple: Clement of Alexandria, *Stromata* 5.9 (PG 9:112): "Palin ho Mōusēs . . . hena d'oun neōn hidrysamenos tou Theou monogenē te kosmon . . . kai ton hena, hōs ouk eti tōi Basileidēi dokei, katēngele Theon."

23. "The purpose *[ratio]* of the unity of the temple or tabernacle . . . was to fix in men's minds the unity of the divine faith, God desiring

that sacrifice be made to him in one place only." Aquinas, *Summa theologica* 1a2æ, 102.4; Dominican ed., 29:161. On the lack of a centralizing force, see Louis M. O. Duchesne, *Early History of the Christian Church* (London: Murray, 1931), 2:521–26. Cf. note 2 above.

24. Peter Cantor, *Verbum abbreviatum (The Abridged Word)* 29 (PL 205:104, 106–7). The historian Socrates, *Historica ecclesiastica (Ecclesiastical History)* 5.22 (PG 67:625–45), made the same observation in the fifth century.

25. This is the "messe publique," the oldest exemplar of which Louis M. O. Duchesne calls "un cérémonial fort postérieur à l'âge antique." *Origines du culte chrétien,* 2nd ed. (Paris: Thorin, 1898), 154; 5th ed. (1920), 172.

26. Cantor, *The Abridged Word* 29 (PL 205:104, 106–7); so also Hilary, *Treatise on the Psalms* 14.3 (PL 9:301).

27. Hilary, *Treatise on the Psalms* 14.3 (PL 9:301); Eusebius, *Preparation for the Gospel* 5.1 (PG 21:312); Jerome, *Commentary on Isaiah* 13.47 (PL 24:471–72); Leo Magnus, *Sermo (Discourse)* 59.8 (PL 54:341); Chrysostom, *Contra Judaeos et Gentiles, quod Christus sit Deus (Against the Jews and the Gentiles, That Christ Is God)* 12 (PG 48:829–30); cf. Chrysostom, *De cruce et latrone (On the Cross and the Thief)* 2.1 (PG 49:409); Chrysostom, *De capto Eutropio et de divitiarum vanitate (On the Capture of Eutropius and the Vanity of Wealth)* 15 (PG 52:410).

28. See the discussion by A. le Nourry in PG 9:900–902. A writing attributed to Athanasius admits that the multiplication of shrines presents "a strange and paradoxical problem"—*xenon kai paradoxon to eperōtema*—to which the author gives an even stranger solution. See *Quaestiones ad Antiochum Ducem (Questions to Duke Antiochus)* 26 (PG 28:613).

29. The temple represents the world—*ho naos de hōs oikos Theou holon ton kosmon typoi,* and since there ̣s but "one world, above and below . . . analogous to the order of the Church," the church itself is

one temple which *ho archiereus monos syn tois hierōmenois eis-erchetai;* Symeon Thessalonicensis, *De sacro templo (On the Holy Temple)* 131 (PG 155:337–40). Cf. Leo, *Discourse* 54.8 (PL 54: 341); Hilary, *Treatise on the Psalms* 121 (PL 9:662–63); and Theodoret, *Treatment of Greek Illnesses* 6 (PG 83:989).

30. Fulgentius, *Contra Fabianum (Against Fabian)* 34 (PL 65:811–12); Photius, *Epistolae (Letters)* 1.8.31 (PG 102:665); Wolbero, *Commentaria in Canticum Canticorum (Commentary on the Song of Solomon)* 3.5.15 (PL 195:1203).

31. Aquinas, *Summa theologica* 1a2æ, 102.4; Dominican ed., 29:161: "Et ideo, ut firmaretur in animis hominum fides unitatis divi-nae, voluit Deus ut in uno loco tantum sibi sacrificium offerretur. . . . Sed cultus novae legis . . . Deo acceptus," etc.

32. Ibid., articuli iv and v. Thomas himself at the beginning of articulus iv refutes the common doctrine of a purely spiritual temple.

33. Anastasius Bibliothecarius, *Historia de vitis romanorum pontificum (History of the Lives of the Roman Pontiffs)* 112, about Stephen VI (PL 128:1399).

34. August Neander, *The Life of Jesus Christ,* 4th ed. (New York: Harper, 1858), 180–81.

35. Charles M. Laymon, *Life and Teachings of Jesus* (New York: Abingdon, 1955), 280.

36. Leo, *Discourse* 3 (PL 54:145).

37. Frederick C. Grant, *An Introduction to New Testament Thought* (New York: Abingdon-Cokesbury, 1950), 14.

38. Barnabas, *Epistola catholica (Catholic Epistle)* 16 (PG 2:771–76). Cf. TB *Yebamot* 6b: "loʾ mim-miqdāš ʿattāh mityārēʾ ʾelleʾ mimmî še-hizhîr ʿal ham-miqdāš." While the temple was still standing, the principle had been established that the efficacy of every species of expiation was morally conditioned. Moore, quoted in William D. Davies, *Paul and Rabbinic Judaism* (London: Society for the Pro-motion of Christian Knowledge, 1948), 257.

39. "Neque enim domum incusabat [Jesus] . . . sed eos, qui non bene utebantur domo." Irenaeus, *Against Heresies* 4.2.6 (PG 7:978). Even Stephen's sermon (Acts 7), usually viewed as an attack on the temple, is rather an appeal for a proper sense of values. See William Manson, *The Epistle to the Hebrews* (London: Hodder and Stoughton, 1951), 28, 30, 34.

40. Quotations from Origen, *Commentaria in Evangelium secundum Matthaeum (Commentary on Matthew)* 14.22–23 (PG 13:1452–53), and *Commentaria in Evangelium Joannis (Commentary on John)* 10.16 (PG 14:349). The temple is built of simplicity, intellect, *veritas, pudicitia, continentia,* etc. Zeno, *Tractate* 1.14 (PL 11:361–62). The theme is extremely popular with theologians.

41. Jewish and Christian doctors alike "spun out abstract doctrines far beyond the ken of the common folk, and insisted that these are the truths of religion and morality. Nor are we closing the gap today." Max Kadushin, *The Rabbinic Mind* (New York: Jewish Theological Seminary of America, 1952), 87–88. "The fathers," says Edward Gibbon, "deem themselves secure and invulnerable behind the ample veil of allegory, which they carefully spread over every tender part of the Mosaic dispensation." Edward Gibbon, *The Decline and Fall of the Roman Empire* (New York: Modern Library, 1932), 1:393 n. 31.

42. Origen, *Commentary on John* 10.20 (PG 14:369–70). *Amphotera mentoige, to te hieron kai to sōma tou Iēsou*—it is quite possible for it to be two or more things at once.

43. Cyril of Alexandria, *Commentarius in Michaeam prophetam (Commentary on Micah)* 4.1.2 (PG 71:644). Cf. Symeon, *On the Holy Temple* 128 (PG 155:336); Photius, *Contra Manichaeos (Against the Manichaeans)* 2 (PG 102:108).

44. Thus Rupert, *Liber Regum (Commentary on Kings)* 3.6–29 (PL 167:1147–75); Hugh of St. Victor, *Allegoriae in Vetus Testamentum (Allegories on the Old Testament)* 3.9 (PL 175:661–63); Hugh of St.

Victor, *De claustro animae (On the Fortress of the Soul)* 3.17 (PL 176:1118–20); Alan of Lille, *Sententiae,* no. 16, 22 (PL 210:236–37, 240); Garnerus, "De Templo" ("On the Temple"), in *Gregorianum* 13.8 (PL 193:398–400); Adam of St. Victor, *Sermones (Sermons)* 40 (PL 198:363–71).

45. See notes 152–57 below.

46. Hilary, *Treatise on the Psalms* 126 (PL 9:694–95). Cf. Olmstead, *Jesus in the Light of History,* 69.

47. "From the beginning the destruction of the Temple and the eventual cessation of the sacrifices had been anticipated." Grant, *Introduction to New Testament Thought,* 14. As early as 587 B.C. "the old dogma that it was blasphemy even to speak of the destructibility of the temple was shattered." Raisin, *Gentile Reactions to Jewish Ideals,* 82.

48. In the *Odes of Solomon* the temple is "préexistant au monde et, de plus, il subsiste hors du monde." Pierre Batiffol, "Les odes de Salomon," *Revue biblique* 20 n.s. 8 (1911): 40. "Est ergo altare in coelis, et templum." Irenaeus, *Against Heresies* 4.18 (PG 7:1024–29). Cf. Davies, *Paul and Rabbinic Judaism,* 162 n. 2.

49. L. J. Liebereich, "Compilation of the Book of Isaiah," *Jewish Quarterly Review* 46 (1956): 272. See *Testament of Levi* 14–18, *Testament of Benjamin* 9, and *Testament of Naphtali* 4.

50. Barnabas, *Catholic Epistle* 16 (PG 2:771–76). That *paradōsei* here means "remove," "take out of circulation," is clear from parallel passages in Matthew 24:9 and *Didache* 16.4; cf. Robert H. Charles, *The Book of Enoch* (Oxford: Oxford University Press, 1912), 198–204.

51. Hilary, *Treatise on the Psalms* 14 (PL 9:301–2): "Sed mons Domini nullus in terra est: omnis enim terra jam pridem per vitia hominum maledictis obnoxia est."

52. Athanasius, *Quaestiones in Pauli epistolas (Questions on the Epistles of Paul)* 127 (PG 28:769); Peter Damian, *Dialogus inter Judaeum et Christianum (Dialogue between a Jew and a Christian)* 9

(PL 145:59); Rupert, *Liber in Numeros (Commentary on Numbers)* 2.21 (PL 167:901); Richard of St. Victor, *On the Tabernacle* 1 (PL 196:212); Richard of St. Victor, *Adnotationes mysticae in Psalmos (Mystic Comments on Psalms)* 28 (PL 196:306); Richard of St. Victor, *In Apocalypsim Joannis (Commentary on the Apocalypse of John)* 7.2 (PL 196:860); Aquinas, *Summa theologica* 1a2æ, 102.4, conclusion; Andrew of Caesarea, *Commentarius in Apocalypsin (Commentary on the Apocalypse of John)* 21.3–4 (PG 106:425); Wolbero, *Commentary on the Song of Solomon* 4 (PL 195:1275).

53. For Tertullian the glory of the temple was extinguished by the mere declaration of the Lord that it was a den of thieves. *De pudicitia (On Modesty)* 1 (PL 2:1033–34). It was not the money changers as such, but really the Jews, that Christ was expelling forever, according to Cyril of Alexandria, *Commentarius in Amos prophetam (Commentary on Amos)* 19 (PG 71:443–44); Leo, *Sermones attributi (Attributed Discourses)* 14 (PL 54:507); Rupert, *Commentarius in Zachariam prophetam (Commentary on Zechariah)* 2.5 (PL 168:735–36), and *Commentary on Amos* 2.3–4 (PL 168:301). For Ernst W. Hengstenberg, *Christology of the Old Testament,* 2nd ed. (Edinburgh: Clark, 1856–58), 4:248, the "den of thieves" verdict "rendered the continuance of the former [temple] absolutely impossible."

54. "Evidens . . . translatio." Leo, *Discourse* 68.3 (PL 54:374).

55. "Nun de . . . eisi hoi pōlountes kai agorazontes en tōi hierōi . . . kai oudamou Iēsous epiphainetai hina ekbalōn sōsēi tous loipous." Origen, *Commentary on Matthew* 16.21 (PG 13:1444–45, 1417, 1448): "All' eithe eiselthōn eis to hieron tou Patros . . . kataballoi Iēsous tas . . . trapezas." Cf. Origen, *Homiliae in Jeremiam (Homilies on Jeremiah)* 9 (PG 13:348). Cf. Gregorius Magnus (Gregory the Great), *Epistolae (Letters)* 11.46 (PL 77:1166); Theophylactus, *Enarratio in Marcum (Commentary on the Gospel of Mark)* 11.15–18 (PG 123:616); Photius, *Against the Manichaeans* 4.23 (PG 102:229); Alcuin, *Commentaria in Sancti Joannis Evangelium (Commentary on John)* 2.4.14–15 (PL 100:773).

56. Photius, *Against the Manichaeans* 4.23 (PG 102:229); so Cyril of Jerusalem, *Catechetical Lecture on the Father* 7 (PG 33:612).

57. Thus Hippolytus, *Demonstratio adversus Judaeos (Against the Jews)* 7 (PG 10:792); Juvencus, *Evangelica historia (Gospel History)* 4.75–80 (PL 19:286–87). This prophecy was "the final 'Let us depart hence' of retiring Deity," according to Frederic W. Farrar, *The Life of Christ* (New York: Cassell, 1903), 2:255, who notes that thirty-five years *later* Deity finally departed! "Those few words completed the prophecy of Israel's desolation." Isidore O'Brien, *The Life of Christ* (Paterson, N.J.: St. Anthony Guild, 1937), 418; 4th ed., 472.

58. Vincent Taylor, *Jesus and His Sacrifice* (London: Macmillan, 1937), 71.

59. So Jerome, *Commentary on Isaiah* 15.52 (PL 24:513–24). Leo, *Discourse* 68 (PL 54:374); Theophanes, *Homilia (Homily)* 27 (PG 132:600). A. Feuillet, "Le sens du mot parousie dans l'évangile de Matthieu," in Davies and Daube, *Background of the New Testament*, 268.

60. Cassiodorus, *Expositio in Psalterium (Commentary on the Psalms)* 21 (PL 70:158); Rupert, *Commentarius in Apocalypsim Joannis (Commentary on the Apocalypse of John)* 9.15 (PL 169:1111); Jerome, *Commentary on Isaiah* 14.52 (PL 24:498); Aquinas, *Summa theologica* 1a2æ, 102.4; Clarence T. Craig, *The Beginning of Christianity* (New York: Abingdon-Cokesbury, 1943), 183. For a more recent treatment, see Dennis Sylva, "The Temple Curtain and Jesus' Death in the Gospel of Luke," *Journal of Biblical Literature* 105 (1986): 239–50.

61. Farrar, *Life of Christ*, 1:194–95. Some scholars find the passage too hot to handle and declare it to be "not in the original utterance of Jesus," but "the travesty of the false witness." Benjamin W. Robinson, *Jesus in Action* (New York: Macmillan, 1942), 77.

62. Gibbon, *Decline and Fall*, 1:393 n. 31; cf. Raisin, *Gentile Reactions to Jewish Ideals*, 31.

63. Quotation from Gordon Leff, "In Search of the Millennium," *Past and Present* 13 (April 1958): 92.

64. Many writers present Jesus as a would-be restorer of temple worship, with the temple as his headquarters. Thus Arthur C. Headlam, *Jesus Christ in History and Faith* (London: Murray, 1925), 137–39; Rudolf K. Bultmann, *Theologie des Neuen Testaments*, 4th ed. (Tübingen: Mohr, 1961), 1:17; cf. English translation, *Theology of the New Testament*, trans. Kendrick Grobel (New York: Scribner, 1951); Benjamin W. Bacon, *Studies in Matthew* (New York: Holt, 1930), 242–43.

65. "Recent research has shown that prophets had a regular part in the temple cultus." Millar Burrows, *Outline of Biblical Theology* (Philadelphia: Westminster, 1946), 255.

66. For a comprehensive statement, see James Strahan, "Temple," in *Dictionary of the Apostolic Church*, ed. James Hastings (New York: Scribner's Sons, 1916–22), 2:556–57; and Brandon, *Fall of Jerusalem*, 21, 29, 39, 127, 263, even vindicating Stephen's position, 89, 127–29, 263.

67. Nils A. Dahl, "Christ, Creation, and the Church," in Davies and Daube, *Background of the New Testament*, 430–31, 424. Quotation is from Krister Stendahl, "Implications of Form Criticism and Tradition-Criticism for Biblical Interpretation," *Journal of Biblical Literature* 77 (1958): 36–37.

68. For closely paralleled Jewish, Christian, and classical concepts, see Bernhard Kötting, *Peregrinatio Religiosa* (Münster: Regensberg, 1950), 57–69, 287–88. The familiar temple imagery in Christian liturgy was disseminated directly by pilgrims coming from Jerusalem. Anton Baumstark, *Abendländische Palästinapilger* (Cologne: Bachen, 1906), 31, 80–83.

69. Charles K. Barrett, "The Eschatology of the Epistle to the Hebrews," in Davies and Daube, *Background of the New Testament*, 382.

70. F.-M. Abel, "Jérusalem," in *Dictionnaire d'archéologie chrétienne et de liturgie*, ed. Fernand Cabrol and Henri Leclerq (Paris: Letouzey et Ané, 1907), 7:2311; cf. Sulpicius Severus, *Historia sacra (Sacred History)* 2.48 (PL 20:156–57), and note 10 above.

71. Gregorius Nyssenus, *Epistolae (Letters)* 2.3 (PG 46:1012–13, 1016); Basil the Great, *Moralia*, Regula 67 (PG 31:808; cf. PG

31:805); Chrysostom, *Ad populum Antiochenum (To the People of Antioch)* 17 (PG 49:177–80); and Chrysostom, *Homily on the Holy Pentecost* 1 (PG 50:453–64).

72. Quotation is from Charles N. Cochrane, *Christianity and Classical Culture* (Oxford: Oxford University Press, 1940), 211; for the concept, see Eusebius, *De laudibus Constantini (In Praise of Constantine)* 4–6 and 10 (PG 20:1332–52, 1372–76).

73. For a discussion, see Michael S. Seidlmayer, "Rom und Romgedanke im Mittelalter," *Saeculum* 7 (1956): 395–412.

74. See Hugh W. Nibley, "The Hierocentric State," in *The Ancient State* (Salt Lake City: Deseret Book and FARMS, 1991), 99–147. W. F. Albright sees in Solomon's temple "a rich cosmic symbolism which was largely lost in later Israelite and Jewish tradition." William F. Albright, *Archaeology and the Religion of Israel* (Baltimore: Johns Hopkins Press, 1942), 154–55; cf. 88–89, 167.

75. Eusebius, *In Praise of Constantine* 4–6 and 10 (PG 20:1332–52, 1372–76); and *De Vita Constantini (On the Life of Constantine)* 3.33–39 (PG 20:1093–1100); 4.60 (PG 20:1209–12).

76. Contemporaries hail him as "the new Bezeliel or Zerubabel, who builds . . . blessed temples of . . . Christ." Antiochus Monachus, *Prologus* (PG 89:1428).

77. Eusebius, *Ecclesiastical History* 10.4.45–46 (PG 20:876–77).

78. So Zeno, *Tractate* 1.14 (PL 11:354–62); Jerome, *Commentary on Isaiah* 1.2.9 (PL 24:49); 17 (PL 24:593); and Jerome, *Epistolae (Letters)* 52.10 (PL 22:535); 130.14 (PL 22:1119); 46–47 (PL 22:492).

79. Eusebius, *Ecclesiastical History* 10.4.45–46 (PG 20:876–77): "hōs mēketi logon, all' ergon gegonenai tēn anō lechtheisan prophēteian [Haggai 2:9], gegonen gar kai nun hōs alēthōs estin."

80. See the editor's enthusiastic comment on the oratory of Paulinus, *Appendix operum Sancti Paulini (Appendix to the Works of Saint Paulinus)* (PL 61:929).

81. Abel, "Jérusalem," 2312, for the timing. It is Zonaras, *Annales (Annals)* 11.23 (PG 134:996), who locates the Roman temple, following

Socrates, *Ecclesiastical History* 1.17 (PG 67:117–21). According to Eusebius, *On the Life of Constantine* 3.28 (PG 20:1088–89), as the digging proceeded, "to semnon kai panagion tēs sōtēriou anastaseōs martyrion par' elpida pasan anephaineto, kai to te hagion tōn hagiōn antron tēn homoian tes tou Sōtēros anabiōseōs apelambanen eikona." That this is not a mere parallelism is indicated by the *kai . . . te* and *homoian.*

82. Eusebius, *On the Life of Constantine* 3.33 (PG 20:1093): *kai dē tou pantos hōsper tina kephalēn, prōtōn hapantōn to hieron antron,* etc., noting that this was the very New Jerusalem that had been foretold by the prophets—an eschatological structure. Cf. Socrates, *Ecclesiastical History* 1.17 (PG 67:117–21).

83. Theodoret, *Explanatio in Ezechielem (Explanation of Ezekiel)* 48.35 (PG 81:1253).

84. Chrysostom, *Sermo post reditum ab exsilio (Discourse following the Return from Exile)* 2 (PG 52:440); "Ubi aedificabo? Absolutum est templum." He is rejoicing that the growth of the church has burst all old traditional bounds such as the limitations of the temple. Cf. Chrysostom, *Interpretatio in Isaiam prophetam (On Isaiah)* 2.3 (PG 56:30, 97); Chrysostom, *Homilia in Sanctum Ignatium Martyrem (Homily on St. Ignatius the Martyr)* 5 (PG 50:595–96); Basil, *Regulae fusius tractatae (Detailed Rules)* 40 (PG 31:1020); Theodoret, *Epistolae (Letters)* 66–68 (PG 83:1236–37); Zeno, *Liber (Commentary)* 2, *Tractate* 46 (PL 11:520–21). Significantly, the most brilliant of these gatherings is for the feast of the Maccabees, that is, to commemorate the rededication of the temple. Chrysostom, *Homilia in sanctos Maccabeos (Homily on the Holy Maccabees)* 1 (PG 50:617–24).

85. Chrysostom, *To the People of Antioch* 17 (PG 49:177–78); Chrysostom, *Against the Jews and the Gentiles* 9 (PG 48:825–26); Gregorius Nyssenus, *Letters* 17 (PG 46:1064).

86. Constantine Manassis, *Compendium Chronicum (A Compendium of Chronicles)* 3267–83 (PG 127:342–43). It was a conscious imitation of Constantine's "New Jerusalem." Procopius, *Buildings* 1,

discussed in the footnotes to Eusebius, *The Life of Constantine* (PG 20:1098–99 nn. 13–14).

87. The story is told in Raisin, *Gentile Reactions to Jewish Ideals,* 361.

88. On Constantinople as the New House of God, see Andras Alföldi, *The Conversion of Constantine and Pagan Rome* (Oxford: Oxford University Press, 1948), 110.

89. Seidlmayer, "Rom und Romgedanke," 400–403. Cf. Pliny, *Letter to Maximus* 8.24.3.

90. See notes 26–28 above. For some amusing arguments, see also Rupert, *De victoria verbi Dei (On the Victory of the Word of God)* 10.10 (PL 169:1430); Peter Damian, *Dialogue between a Jew and a Christian* 10 (PL 145:60–61).

91. Eusebius, *On the Life of Constantine* 4.24 (PG 20:1172); 4.42 (PG 20:1189–90).

92. So Seidlmayer, "Rom und Romgedanke," 402–3.

93. Thus in *Attributed Discourses* 14.4–5 (PL 54:507), Leo says that the *cathedra* occupied by Moses has been torn down *mystice* and become a *pestilentiae Cathedram,* the change occurring at the moment Jesus drove the money changers from the *temple.*

94. Seidlmayer, "Rom und Romgedanke," 402.

95. Ibid., 409. See Cochrane, *Christianity and Classical Culture,* chap. 5.

96. Leo, *Attributed Discourses* 16; 17.1–2 (PL 54:511–13); Jerome, *Commentary on Isaiah* 1.2.9 (PL 24:49): "Ubi quondam erat templum et religio Dei, ibi Adriani statua et Jovis idolum collocatum," which many Christians regard as literal fulfillment of Mark 13:14.

97. "Partim ignorantiae vitio, partim paganitatis spiritu." Leo, *Discourse* 27.4 (PL 54:218–19); cf. 89.4 (PL 54:446).

98. Ibid., 40.5 (PL 54:271); 48.1 (PL 54:298); 49.1 (PL 54:301); 60.3 (PL 54:344); 21.3 and 22.1–2 (PL 54:192–95); 23.5 (PL 54:203); 88.4–5 and 89.1–2 (PL 54:442–46).

99. Ibid., 3.1–3 (PL 54:145–56); 5.3 (PL 54:154).

100. "Nihil legalium institutionum, nihil propheticarum resedit figurarum, quod non totum in Christi sacramenta transierit. Nobiscum est signaculum circumcisionis . . . nobiscum puritas sacrificii, baptismi veritas, honor templi." Ibid., 66 (PL 54:365–66); cf. 30.3 (PL 54:229). It was all too good for the Jews.

101. Ibid., 4.1–2 (PL 54:149). Erich Caspar, *Geschichte des Papsttums von den Anfängen bis zur Höhe der Weltherrschaft* (Tübingen: Mohr, 1930) 1:403; Seidlmayer, "Rom und Romgedanke," 403.

102. The *Hauptthema* of this long writing is that the house of God is "non terrena et caduca." Hilary, *Treatise on the Psalms* 121.2 (PL 9:661–62); in fact, if one accepts the temple passages literally, then "inanis est psalmus, et mendax Propheta!" Ibid., 124.2 (PL 9:680).

103. Ambrose (dubia), *De sacramentis (On the Sacraments)* 1.4 (PL 16:420); 4.3 (PL 16:438; cf. PL 16:421). Chapter 4 is intensely invidious.

104. Jerome, *Letters* 46 (PL 22:486).

105. Chrysostom, *In Epistolam ad Hebraeos (On the Epistle to the Hebrews)* 12.32 (PG 63:221).

106. Chrysostom, *De sanctis martyribus (On the Holy Martyrs)* 1 (PG 50:645–56; cf. PG 50:582). This is a favorite theme with Chrysostom.

107. Chrysostom, *De sacerdotio (On the Priesthood)* 3.4 (PG 48:642). Carl Seltmann in his edition (Münster: Schöningh, 1887), 83–84, raises the knotty question of just how literal all this is supposed to be.

108. Methodius, *Convivium decem virginum (Banquet of the Ten Virgins)* 7 (PG 18:109).

109. "Ibi enim stamus mentis oculos figimus . . . humana mens . . . superiora illa atque coelestia utcunque in aenigmate conspicit." Garner, *On the Temple* 8.8.7 (PL 193:397; cf. PL 193:936); Zeno, *Tractate* 2.63 (PL 11:518–19); Eusebius, *Ecclesiastical History* 10.4, passim (PG 20:848–80).

110. Friedrich A. Müller, *Der Islam im Morgen- und Abendland* (Berlin: Grote, 1885–87), 1:285; Raisin, *Gentile Reactions to Jewish Ideals,* 370.

111. Eutychius, *Annales (Annals)* 287–92 (PG 111:1100).

112. Gustav E. von Grunebaum, *Muhammadan Festivals* (New York: Schuman, 1951), 20.

113. "If Islam substituted the Kibla of Mecca for that of Jerusalem, on the other hand it renders the greatest honor to the site of the temple . . . and pure monotheism rebuilt its fortress on Mt. Moriah," wrote Renan, quoted in Raisin, *Gentile Reactions to Jewish Ideals,* 389.

114. Adam Mez, *Renaissance des Islams* (Heidelberg: Winter, 1903), 302. Cf. English translation by Salahuddin Bukhish (London: Luzac, 1937).

115. Mez, *Renaissance des Islams,* 302–3.

116. Müller, *Der Islam im Morgen- und Abendland,* 1:285.

117. Just as the Christians turned the temple site into a *sterquilinium* (note 161 below), so the Muslims just as childishly called the Church of the Holy Sepulchre not *al-qiyāma,* but *al-qumāma,* that is, *sterquilinium!* Ernst Rosenmüller, ed., *Idrīsī's Syria* (Leipzig: Sumtibus Io Ambros Barthii, 1828), 10 n. 36. Though at the end of the tenth century Christians still execrated the temple site, Eutychius, *Annals* 287–92 (PG 111:1100), in the thirteenth century a friend of the sultan was rudely barred from the place, being told: "such things are not revealed to such as you. Do not insult our Law!" "Mithla hādhihi al-ʾumūri lā takhfā ʿalā ʾamthālika. Lā tabṭul namūsanā!" etc. Al-Qazwīnī, *Kosmographie,* ed. Ferdinand Wüstenfeld (Göttingen: Dieterich, 1848), 2:109.

118. Fulcher, *Historia Hierosolymitana* 1.26.9, with editorial discussion by Heinrich Hagenmeyer in his edition, *Fulcheri Carnotensis historia Hiersolymitana* (Heidelberg: Winter, 1913), 290–91.

119. Müller, *Der Islam im Morgen- und Abendland,* 2:135.

120. Guibert, *Gesta Dei per Francos (Acts of God through the Franks)* 7.10 (PL 156:795); Fulcher, *History Hierosolymitana* 1.27.12–13. See note 133 below. For the Muslim reaction, see Müller, *Der Islam im Morgen- und Abendland,* 2:157.

121. Athanasius, *Questions to Duke Antiochus* 44 (PG 28:625).

122. Aetheria (Silvia), *Peregrinatio ad loca sancta (Pilgrimage to Holy Places),* 4th ed. (Heidelberg: Heraeus, 1939), 37:3; 48:1–2; 49:1.

123. Ibid., 26.

124. She compares the pilgrims to those who anciently came to Jerusalem to hear the law (ibid., 27:1, 6) and notes that fasting was forbidden on the Temple Mount and there only (ibid., 44:1) rather than at New Testament shrines. An even earlier pilgrim, Melito of Sardis, describes a strictly Old Testament pilgrimage to the East, *Fragmentum (Fragment)* (PG 5:1216).

125. Photius, *Against the Manichaeans* 2.11 (PG 102:109); cf. Raisin, *Gentile Reactions to Jewish Ideals,* 31.

126. Edwyn C. Hoskyns, *The Fourth Gospel,* ed. Francis N. Davey (London: Faber and Faber, 1940), 1:202–3; Phythian-Adams, *The People and the Presence,* 74.

127. H. B. Swete, quoted by Barrett, "Eschatology of the Epistle to the Hebrews," 383. Revelation 21:21–27.

128. Titus Tobler, *Dr. Titus Toblers zwei Bücher Topographie von Jerusalem* (Berlin: Reimer, 1853–54), 1:540ff. Origen, *Commentary on John* 10.22 (PG 14:377–78), comments on the "inconsistency and confusion" of the records. Cf. Socrates, *Ecclesiastical History* 1.17 (PG 67:117–21); Sozomen, *Historica ecclesiastica (Ecclesiastical History)* 1.1 (PG 67:929–33); Eusebius, *On the Life of Constantine* 3.28 (PG 20:1088–89). Even the holy sites of Galilee had been transported to Jerusalem at an early time. Brandon, *Fall of Jerusalem,* 197–98.

129. "The place where the dream of Jacob occurred is the place where Adam was created, namely, the place of the future Temple and the center of the earth." Andreas Altmann, "The Gnostic Background of the Rabbinic Adam Legends," *Jewish Quarterly Review* 35 (1945):

390–91. But "the Midrash also teaches . . . that Adam dwelt on Mt. Moriah and there 'returned to the earth from which he was taken.'" Robert Eisler, *Iesous basileus ou basileusas* (Heidelberg: Winter, 1930), 1:523. Yet the place where Adam sleeps is Golgotha, the foot of the cross resting on his skull. Epiphanius, *Adversus haereses (Against Heresies)* 2.1.4–5 (PG 41:844), and many others. Christian and Muslim traditions place the holy of holies on the rock on which Abraham offered Isaac. Rupert, *Liber Genesis (Commentary on Genesis)* 6.28–29 (PL 167:427–28), making it the logical spot for the supreme culminating sacrifice of the cross. Cf. Aquinas, *Summa theologica* 1a2æ, 102.4.2: "Et tunc primo aedificatum fuit templum, in loco quem designaverat Abraham . . . ad immolandum," etc. Both Fulcher and Saewulf report as eyewitnesses that the original ark of the covenant reposed directly in the center of the Church of the Holy Sepulchre; cited by Hagenmeyer in *Fulcheri Carnotensis,* 287–88. The Arabic writers are equally confusing: al-Qazwīnī, *Kosmographie,* 2:107–9; Ibn Ajjās, "Geography," in *Chrestomathia Arabica,* ed. Friedrich Arnold (Halle: Pfeffer, 1853), 1:64–66; Rosenmüller, *Idrīsī's Syria,* 9–12; Ibn Baṭuṭa, *Muhadhdhib rihlat Ibn Batutah* (Cairo: al-Matbaᶜah al-Amiriyah, 1938), 1:33–34.

130. See William Simpson, "The Middle of the World, in the Holy Sepulchre," *Palestine Exploration Fund Quarterly* (1888): 260–63; C. M. Watson, "The Traditional Sites on Sion," *Palestine Exploration Fund Quarterly* (1910): 209; C. M. Watson, trans., "Commemoratorium de casis dei vel monasteriis," *Palestine Exploration Fund Quarterly* (1913): pl. iii, opp. p. 28. The seal of King Baldwin of Jerusalem shows the two buildings as almost identical domes, side by side within a single walled enclosure.

131. Fulcher, *History Hierosolymitana* 1.30.4.

132. "It was another, a new creation!" cries Raimundus de Angiles, *Historia Francorum qui ceperunt Hierusalem* (Philadelphia: American Philosophical Society, 1968), 330–31; cited by Hagenmeyer in Fulcher, *History Hierosolymitana* 1.30.4.

133. J. Casper Barth (1720), quoted by Hagenmeyer in *Fulcheri Carnotensis,* 287.

134. The materials are given and discussed in ibid., 285–87, 304–6.

135. The treaty of 1229 allowed the Christians possession of the sepulchre, while the Muslims retained the *Templum Domini,* that is, the distinction was clearly preserved. Charles Diehl, *Le Monde oriental de 395 à 1081* (Paris: Presses universitaire de France, 1944), 462.

136. See the long article in the *Enciclopedia Universal Ilustrada* (Madrid: Espasa-Calpe, 1928), 60:727–41. The rules of the order closely resemble those of some Jewish sectaries; cf. Henri Daniel-Rops, *L'église de la cathédrale et de la croisade* (Paris: Fayard, 1952), 145, 718, 720, 730; cf. English translation by John Warrington, *Cathedral and Crusade* (New York: Dutton, 1957). It is not surprising that the order was accused of heresy since it "urged the emigration of converts to Palestine to help prophecy to become fulfilled." E. Kautzsch, cited by Emil Kraeling, *The Old Testament since the Reformation* (New York: Harper, 1955), 133.

137. See, for instance, Duchesne, *Origines du culte chrétien,* 45; 5th ed., 47. Cf. John Ward, "The Fall of the Templars," *Journal of Religious History* 13 (1984): 92–113, for an overview of contemporary research.

138. S. Krauss, "The Jews in the Works of the Church Fathers," *Jewish Quarterly Review* 6 (1893–94): 238, who paraphrases Rufinus, *Invectio (Attack)* 1.5 and 2.589: "If a few Jews were to institute new rites, the Church would have to follow suit and immediately adopt them."

139. William Oesterly and Theodore Robinson, *An Introduction to the Books of the Old Testament* (New York: Macmillan, 1934), 194; cf. Louis Finkelstein, "The Origin of the Synagogue," *Proceedings of the American Academy for Jewish Research* 3 (1930): 49–59.

140. Hilary, *Treatise on the Psalms* 137 (PL 9:787). Symeon, *Expositio de divino templo (Exposition on the Holy Temple)* 2 (PG 155:701),

describes the mass in terms of the temple. See Malachi 1:11, the chief scriptural support for the mass. Gustav Oehler, *Theology of the Old Testament* (Grand Rapids: Zondervan, 1883), 519–20, deals only with the temple. Daniel-Rops, *L'église de la cathédrale,* 542–43, points out that the round churches of Europe, revived at the time of the Crusades, were direct imitations of the temple at Jerusalem.

141.   Chrysostom, *In Epistolam II ad Corinthios homilia (Homily on the Second Epistle to the Corinthians)* 2.2 (PG 61:476); Epiphanius, *Against Heresies* 61.8 (PG 41:1049).

142.   Rupert, "De Azymo" ("On Unleavened Bread"), in *De divinis officiis (On Divine Duties)* 2.22 (PL 170:48–51); cf. Epiphanius, *Against Heresies* 30.16 (PG 41:432). Cf. Leo, *Discourse* 92 (PL 54:453).

143.   Caspar Sagittarius, in *Thesaurus antiquitatum Romanarum,* ed. Johannes G. Graevius (Traject. ad Rhenum: Franciscus Halman, 1697) 6:465, 492–93, noting that the Christian veils "procul dubio imitati sunt morem in templo Salomonis."

144.   The place of the altar is a *terribilis locus,* Rupert, *Commentary on Genesis* 7.23–24 (PL 167:468–69); "inaccessible and terrible," Symeon, *Dialogus contra haereses (Dialogue against Heresies)* 21 (PG 155:108), and *Exposition on the Holy Temple* 2 (PG 155:701), citing the case of Ambrose in the West, who barred even the emperor "both from the naos and the altar." Cf. Gregorius Nazianzenus, *Carminum liber I, theologica sectio II, poemata moralia (Moral Poems)* 34.220–65 (PG 37:961); Pachymeros, *De Andronico Palaelogo (On Andronicus Palaelogus)* 1.5 (PG 144:25). In the East only the emperor could enter the tabernacle and only at Easter and his coronation. Codinus, *De officiis Constantinopolitanis (On the Offices at Constantinople)* 17 (PG 157:109–10); cf. Cantacusenus, *Historia* 1.41 (PG 153:280–81); Ivo, *Sermo (Discourse)* 4 (PL 162:532–33). At Constantinople and the Vatican there was even a mark on the pavement, as there had been in the temple court of Jerusalem, to show the point beyond which the vulgar might not pass. Constantine Porphyrogenitus, *De caeremoniis*

aulae Byzantinae (On the Ritual of the Byzantine Court) 1.10 (PG 112:161); see especially the editor's note on this.

145. Clement of Alexandria, *Stromata* 7.7 (PG 9:461), with long note by le Nourry (PG 9:462–63); Hippolytus, *Fragmenta in Jeremiam (On Jeremiah)* (PG 10:632). Other and later sources given by Gronovius, in Graevius, *Thesaurus antiquitatum Romanarum*, 7:160.

146. Ivo, *Discourse* 4 (PL 162:527–35).

147. William K. L. Clarke, *Liturgy and Worship* (New York: Macmillan, 1932), 55–59.

148. Rabanus Maurus, *Expositio super Jeremiam (Exposition on Jeremiah)* 4.7 (PL 111:858).

149. Origen, *Commentaria in Epistolam Pauli ad Romanos (Commentary on the Epistle to the Romans)* 6.7 (PG 14:1073); Zeno, *Tractate* 2.66 (PL 11:520–21); Methodius, *Banquet of the Ten Virgins* 5.9.1 (PG 18:177); Paulinus of Nola, *Poema (Poem)* 34.337–48 (PL 61:683). With the fall of the temple "a stupor seems to have settled upon the Jews." Brandon, *Fall of Jerusalem*, 165.

150. Athanasius, *Oratio de incarnatione verbi Dei (Oration on the Incarnation of the Word)* 40 (PG 25:165).

151. For Eusebius the mere statement that Jerusalem will be trodden under foot "shows that the temple shall never rise again"; he admits that the text adds "until the time of the Gentiles be fulfilled," but when is that? Eusebius has the answer: It means never! *Theophania (Theophany)* 8 (PG 24:649–50). Athanasius is even more naive: We know (he argues) that Christ was a true Prophet because Jerusalem will never rise again. And how do we know that? Because since all has been fulfilled in the coming of the true Prophet, it cannot rise again! Athanasius, *Oration on the Incarnation of the Word* 39 (PG 25:164–65). Jerome, *Commentary on Isaiah* 1.5 (PL 24:29–30), insists that the words "Non est in eo sanitas" (Isaiah 1:6) refer to the time of Titus and absolutely prove that the temple can never be restored. Even more

far-fetched is Eusebius's demonstration from the thirty pieces of silver, in *Demonstratio evangelica (Proof for the Gospel)* 10 (PG 22:745).

152. Origen, *Contra Celsum (Against Celsus)* 4.22 (PG 11:1056–57): "Tharrountes d' eroumen, hoti oud' apokatastathēsontai." The same argument is employed by Jerome, *Commentary on Isaiah* 1.1 (PL 24:20–22); and Hippolytus, *Fragmenta in Danielem (On Daniel)* 8–22 (PG 10:648–55).

153. Chrysostom, *Against the Jews and the Gentiles* 5 (PG 48:884, 889, 896); cf. Origen, *Against Celsus* 4.22 (PG 11:1057, with a long discussion in PG 11:1056–60), telling how Grotius developed the argument. Hengstenberg, *Christology of the Old Testament*, 3:291–92, makes this the official Protestant party line; cf. Farrar, *Life of Christ*, 2:255–56: "Neither Hadrian nor Julian, nor any other, were able to build upon its site," etc.

154. So Strahan, "Temple," 557.

155. Marcel Simon, *Verus Israel* (Paris: De Boccard, 1964), 118–20, noting, p. 120, that in spite of all efforts to explain it away the danger remains real; cf. trans. H. McKeating (New York: Oxford University Press, 1986), 91–93.

156. Raisin, *Gentile Reactions to Jewish Ideals*, 370. On the usefulness of pagan ruins as object lessons, see Socrates, *Ecclesiastical History* 1.16 (PG 67:116–17).

157. Kraus, "Jews in the Works of the Church Fathers," 227.

158. Jerome, *Commentary on Isaiah* 17.64 (PL 24:650), citing Josephus, *Jewish Antiquities* 6.12, to prove that the temple will never return. Theodoret, *Explanation of Ezekiel* 48 (PG 81:1252–53 and 1760); and Chrysostom, *Against the Jews and the Gentiles* 5 (PG 48:884, 889, 896), express the same impatience. See Kraus, "Jews in the Works of the Church Fathers," 90–91, 240–45, for others.

159. Theophylactus, *Commentary on the Gospel of Mark* 13.1–4 (PG 123:633): "hōste peirōntai deixai pseudē ton Christon."

160. The story is fully treated by Michael Adler, "The Emperor Julian and the Jews," *Jewish Quarterly Review,* orig. ser., 5 (1893): 615–51.

161. Rufinus, *Historica ecclesiastica (Ecclesiastical History)* 1.37 (PL 21:505); Theodoret, *Historica ecclesiastica (Ecclesiastical History)* 3.15 (PG 82:1112).

162. So Theodoret, *Ecclesiastical History* 3.15 (PG 82:1112); Philostorgius, *Ecclesiasticae historiae (Ecclesiastical History)* 7.14 (PG 65:552).

163. Rufinus, *Ecclesiastical History* 1.37 (PL 21:505); Socrates, *Ecclesiastical History* 3.20 (PG 67:428–32).

164. Adler, "The Emperor Julian and the Jews," 649. On the temple as a test case, Chrysostom, *Against the Jews and the Gentiles* 5.3 (PG 48:888); 6.4 (PG 48:909).

165. A blunt statement is that of David M. Stanley, "Kingdom to Church," *Theological Studies* 16 (1955): 26: "The definitive coming of the Church . . . terminates the existence of the Temple."

166. Johannes Hempel, *Die althebräische Literatur und ihr hellenistisch-jüdisches Nachleben* (Potsdam: Athenaion, 1930), 92. A significant point overlooked by commentators.

167. Adler, "The Emperor Julian and the Jews," 637–51.

168. Ferdinand Prat, *Jesus Christ* (Milwaukee: Bruce, 1950), 2:230, hails the fireball story as conclusive proof that Jesus' prophecy of "not one stone upon another . . . has been fulfilled to the letter." The learned le Nourry argues that while the destruction of Jewish and pagan temples by fire, especially lightning, is a sure sign of divine wrath, a like fate suffered by Christian buildings is without significance, since Christians do not believe that God dwells in houses made with hands (note in PG 9:899–901).

169. Athanasius, *Historia Arianorum ad monachos (Arian History)* 71 (PG 25:777): "a persecution, a prelude and a preparation *(prooimion de kai paraskeuē)* for the Antichrist." Cf. ibid., 74 (PG 25:781); 79 (PG 25:789).

170. Quotation from Irenaeus, *Against Heresies* 5.25 (PG 7:1189). Cyril of Jerusalem says it is a dreadful thing to think of but cannot for that reason be denied. *Catechesis XV. de secundo Christi adventu (Catechetical Lectures on the Second Coming of Christ)* 15 (PG 33:889–92).

171. Basil, *Commentarius in Isaiam prophetam (Commentary on Isaiah)* 3.110 (PG 30:296), who for the rest is very partial to a spiritual and intellectual temple (PG 30:289, 233).

172. See notes 165–70 above. In one attempt the workers unearthed a stone bearing the inscription: In the beginning was the Word. "This was proof positive that it is vain ever to try to rebuild [Jerusalem]—evidence of a divine and irrevocable decree that the Temple has vanished forever!" Philostorgius, *Ecclesiastical History* 7.14 (PG 65:552–53).

173. Even Eusebius had his doubts and wondered if the Montanists might be right. Walter Völker, "Von welchen Tendenzen liess sich Eusebius bei Abfassung seiner 'Kirchengeschichte' leiten?" *Vigiliae christianae* 4 (1950): 170.

174. Well expressed in Simon, *Verus Israel*, 118–24.

175. See Helen Rosenau, "The Synagogue and the Diaspora," *Palestine Exploration Fund Quarterly* (1937): 200.

176. Jerome, *Commentary on Isaiah* 17.40 (PL 24:593–94).

177. See Hugh W. Nibley, "The Unsolved Loyalty Problem: Our Western Heritage," in *The Ancient State*, 218–22; and "Victoriosa Loquacitas," in *The Ancient State*, 260–69.

178. Heinrich Bornkamm, *Grundriss zum Studium der Kirchengeschichte* (Gütersloh: Bertelsmann, 1949), 113–14.

179. While Fernand Cabrol, *Les origines liturgiques* (Paris: Letouzey et Ané, 1906), 48–56, strenuously denies that "toute cette splendeur dont le culte fut entouré" was of any but the purest Hebraic origin, such eminent Catholic authorities as Joseph Lechner and Ludwig Eisenhofer, *Liturgik des römischen Ritus* (Freiburg: Herder, 1953), 5–6, think otherwise.

180. Thomas Livius, *St. Peter Bishop of Rome* (London: Burns and Oates, 1888), 521, while boasting that his church alone in Christendom possesses the Holy City, just like the Jews and the Muslims, never mentions the temple but always puts the synagogue in its place. For example, "The divinely appointed Aaronical high-priesthood . . . was in the Synagogue the fountainhead of all other priesthood" (p. 523), and "The once-favored Synagogue . . . had become a widow . . . without altar or sacrifice" (p. 527). Only once does he let slip the ugly little word, and that in a footnote (p. 527), but it is enough to show that he knows better and is deliberately avoiding the embarrassing word, as Christian scholars consistently do.

181. So Gustaf Wingren, "Weg, Wanderung und verwandte Begriffe," *Studia Theologica* 3 (1951): 111–12.

182. "Le Temple est mort à jamais" is the cry of Marcel Simon, "Retour du Christ et reconstruction du temple dans la pensée chrétienne primitive," in *Aux sources de la tradition chrétienne: Mélanges offerts à M. Maurice Goguel* (Neuchâtel: Delachaux and Niestlé, 1950), 252; cf. 253, 257. An interesting development is the admission that the original Christians were devoted to the temple, coupled with a rebuke for their foolishness; so Bultmann, *Theologie des Neuen Testaments,* 1:54, 57, cf. English translation, 53, 57; O'Brien, *Life of Christ,* 418. Cf. Charles Briggs, *Messianic Prophecy* (New York: Scribner's Sons, 1891), 289.

183. Charles H. Dodd, *The Interpretation of the Fourth Gospel* (Cambridge: Cambridge University Press, 1953), 300–301; Barrett, "Eschatology of the Epistle to the Hebrews," 374–76; Burrows, *Outline of Biblical Theology,* 276. Even Farrar, *Life of Christ,* 1:192–93, was very cautious in condemning the temple. Phythian-Adams's whole book, *The People and the Presence,* belongs in this hesitant and compromising group.

184. J. F. Walvoord, "The Doctrine of the Millennium," *Biblioteca sacra* 115 (1958): 106–8. "The entire sacrificial system of the Old

Testament, while perhaps incongruous with western civilization aesthetics, was nevertheless commanded by God himself. . . . If a literal view of the temple and sacrifices be allowed, it provides a more intimate view of worship in the millennium than might otherwise be afforded." Ibid., 107–8.

Index